CERTIFICATE IN BOOKKEEPING

(COMPUTERISED)

Institute of Certified Bookkeepers

Level II

British Library Cataloguing-in-Publication Data

A catalogue record for this book is available from the British Library.

Published by:

Kaplan Publishing UK
Unit 2 The Business Centre
Molly Millars Lane
Wokingham
RG41 2QZ

ISBN 978-1-78415-199-7

© Kaplan Financial Limited, 2014

Printed and bound in Great Britain.

CONTENTS

STUDY TEXT AND WORKBOOK

INTRODUCTION

STUDY TEXT

This study text has been specially prepared for the Institute of Certified Bookkeepers Computerised Bookkeeping Level II qualification.

It uses a case study approach to guide you through the syllabus and builds up your knowledge and skills chapter by chapter. The text is based upon Sage Instant Account V19, but can also be followed if you are using Sage Line 50 or other versions of Sage Instant Accounts.

Syllabus

The Level II Certificate in Bookkeeping covers the basic principles of single and double entry bookkeeping and its application to business in both a manual and a computerised system.

The ICB has stated that the Level II Certificate in Bookkeeping unit is designed to equip students with the knowledge and skills they need for the role of an assistant bookkeeper under supervision. Students should be able to make postings from the books of prime entry and from source documents to the ledger accounts and produce an initial trial balance.

They will also be able to set up a computerised bookkeeping system, enter details of all transactions and produce reports.

This study text covers all the aspects of computerised bookkeeping included in the syllabus.

Manual Bookkeeping for Level II is covered in a separate study text.

Learning objectives

On completion of the Level II Certificate in Bookkeeping, the student will be able to:

- Understand the following areas of underpinning knowledge:
    - The importance of adhering to a code of professional ethics
    - The differences between the structures of different types of businesses
    - The importance of legislation that applies to bookkeepers
    - The basic elements of a contract
    - The accounting equation
    - The concept of reporting on a cash basis for income tax purposes
    - The concept of business entity, duality and historical cost
- Understand banking procedures including the need for security
- Understand the purpose and range of business documents, and accurately prepare them
- Understand the purpose of, and make entries into, the ledgers and books of prime entry including the use of control accounts
- Understand the process of dealing with and accounting for VAT

in the ledgers

- Understand the purpose and use of the two and three-column cash book, the analysed cash book and the petty cash book
- Understand the purpose and use of the trial balance
- Understand when to open a suspense account
- Set up a business in a computerised system
- Process entries into nominal and subsidiary ledger accounts
- Print out reports as follows:
  - Trial balance
  - Audit trail
  - Nominal account transactions
  - Sales and purchase ledger transactions

Learning Outcomes and Assessment criteria

The unit consists of eight Learning Outcomes which are further broken down into Assessment criteria.

Learning Outcome 8 is covered in this study text and Learning Outcomes 1 - 7 are covered in the study text for Manual Bookkeeping at Level II.

Learning Outcome 8 and its Assessment criteria are listed below:

Topic 8 – Use a computerised accounts package	
Learning Outcome	**Assessment Criteria**
8.1 Health and Safety	Be able to: • demonstrate an awareness of the health and safety issues of using computer systems

8.2 Business Set Up	Be able to:
	
	 • access the software
	 • set up the details for a new business to include:
	   – name, address, start-up date, VAT registration
	   – product lines (sales)
	   – VAT rates
	   – set up customer and supplier accounts in

	sales and purchase ledger with details of name, address, credit limit and opening balances where appropriate – extract print outs with all appropriate details – set up accounts to record income and expenditure items and set up nominal codes – set up pro forma for producing sales invoices, credit notes and other documentation
8.3 Processing Nominal Ledger and Subsidiary Ledger Accounts	Be able to: • create entries to record transactions in the appropriate ledger accounts (by use of coding) for: – credit sales and returns (including trade and cash discount) – credit purchases and returns – supplier invoices for goods and services other than purchases – cash sales and cash purchases – payment of supplier invoices (creditors) for purchases, and other goods and services – receipts from customers (debtors) – accounting treatment of entries relating to payroll – accounting treatment of bad debts – treatment of petty cash – sale of fixed assets
8.4 Generate reports	Be able to: • generate and print out the following reports: – trial balance – audit trail – nominal account transactions – bank account transactions – sales and purchase ledger transactions

KAPLAN PUBLISHING

THE ASSESSMENT

The format of the assessment

The assessment takes the form of an online assessment which can be sat at home, and relevant print-outs uploaded to the ICB for assessment. You will need to contact the ICB to register for this exam. You must have your own accounting software package.

Any accounting software package can be used but Microsoft Excel and other spreadsheets are not appropriate. The ICB advise students to exercise caution when using any software trial versions as they may offer restricted functionality, for example, a standard Sage trial version may not permit the user to print out the requisite reports.

Results are posted directly to the student within one calendar month of receipt of a completed answer paper.

If an assessment is not returned within the deadline period, the assessment will be graded as a Fail and the student must apply for a new assessment and pay any necessary fees

The assessment itself takes the form of a case study approach of a fictional company. You will be asked to process transactions for this business, and print out various reports for submission to the ICB. The practice assessment at the back of this study text will give you a very good understanding of what will be expected of you in the real assessment. It is also strongly recommended you purchase an extra mock assessment from the ICB's website as this will closely resemble the format of the real assessment.

STUDY SKILLS

Preparing to study

Devise a study plan

Determine which times of the week you will study.

Split these times into sessions of at least one hour for study of new material. Any shorter periods could be used for revision or practice.

Put the times you plan to study onto a study plan for the weeks from now until the assessment and set yourself targets for each period of study – in your sessions make sure you cover the whole course, activities and the associated questions in the workbook at the back of the manual.

If you are studying more than one qualification at a time, try to vary your subjects as this can help to keep you interested and see subjects as part of wider knowledge.

When working through your course, compare your progress with your plan and, if necessary, re-plan your work (perhaps including extra sessions) or, if you are ahead, do some extra revision / practice questions.

Effective studying

Active reading

You are not expected to learn the text by rote, rather, you must understand what you are reading and be able to use it to pass the assessment and develop good practice.

A good technique is to use SQ3Rs – Survey, Question, Read, Recall, Review:

1   **Survey the chapter**

    Look at the headings and read the introduction, knowledge, skills and content, so as to get an overview of what the chapter deals with.

2   **Question**

    Whilst undertaking the survey ask yourself the questions you hope the chapter will answer for you.

KAPLAN PUBLISHING

3   **Read**

Read through the chapter thoroughly working through the activities and, at the end, making sure that you can meet the learning objectives highlighted on the first page.

4   **Recall**

At the end of each section and at the end of the chapter, try to recall the main ideas of the section / chapter without referring to the text. This is best done after short break of a couple of minutes after the reading stage.

5   **Review**

Check that your recall notes are correct.

You may also find it helpful to re-read the chapter to try and see the topic(s) it deals with as a whole.

Note taking

Taking notes is a useful way of learning, but do not simply copy out the text.

The notes must:

- be in your own words
- be concise
- cover the key points
- well organised
- be modified as you study further chapters in this text or in related ones.

Trying to summarise a chapter without referring to the text can be a useful way of determining which areas you know and which you don't.

Three ways of taking notes

1   **Summarise the key points of a chapter**

2   **Make linear notes**

A list of headings, subdivided with sub-headings listing the key points.

If you use linear notes, you can use different colours to highlight key points and keep topic areas together.

Use plenty of space to make your notes easy to use.

3   **Try a diagrammatic form**

The most common of which is a mind map.

To make a mind map, put the main heading in the centre of the paper and put a circle around it.]

Draw lines radiating from this to the main sub-headings which again have circles around them.

Continue the process from the sub-headings to sub-sub-headings.

Highlighting and underlining

You may find it useful to underline or highlight key points in your study text – but do be selective.

You may also wish to make notes in the margins.

Further reading

In addition to this text, you should also read all the information contained within the ICB's assessment area. It is strongly recommended you purchase an extra mock assessment from the ICB's website.

An introduction to computerised bookkeeping

1

CONTENTS

1 Introduction

The aim of this manual is to guide you through the computerised accounting aspects of your studies.

To complete this manual you will need an understanding of the basics of double entry bookkeeping and a copy of SAGE. There are a number of versions of SAGE; this manual uses SAGE Instant Accounts version 19. If you have another version of SAGE, or even another accounting package, you should still be able to proceed without too much difficulty, although you may find that some of the screen-shots used in the manual differ.

The manual uses a case study approach to guide you step-by-step. It assumes that you have never used a computerised accounting package before. Even if you have, it is worth starting at the beginning to ensure that you don't 'jump ahead' too quickly.

2 Manual and computerised bookkeeping

The double entry system of bookkeeping that is still used today was developed in Italy in the fifteenth century. With the introduction of affordable and reliable information technology in the last thirty years, it was perhaps inevitable that business organisations would look to find ways to computerise their bookkeeping systems. Now it is rare to find an organisation which does not use some form of computer to aid in the day-to-day record keeping that is an essential aspect of running a business, whether large or small.

For very small organisations, a simple spreadsheet to record monies in and out of the business may suffice. However, once a business becomes larger or more complex, it may be beneficial to introduce a computerised bookkeeping system. There are many proprietary versions on the market, each of which works in a similar way but which will offer different approaches to data entry, presentation of reports and so on, as well as different 'extras' such as stock management modules, budgeting and tax planning. Some systems also allow a company to integrate a computerised payroll function.

3 Benefits of a computerised system

The main benefits ascribed to a computerised bookkeeping system are:

- Quicker, more efficient processing of data

- Fewer mathematical errors – because the system completes all the double entry and other mathematical functions (e.g. calculation of percentages) there is reduced opportunity for human error

- Accounting documents (e.g. invoices, statements etc.) can be generated automatically, using tailored documents designed to incorporate company details, logos etc.

- The range of information that can be easily produced in reports is wide and varied, meaning businesses can report to various internal and external groups (e.g. management, directors, shareholders, banks etc.) in an appropriate format

- There is no need for manual processing of data – computerised bookkeeping systems complete all the double entry automatically

- Hardware and software prices have fallen dramatically over the last thirty years, making a computerised system affordable to all organisations

- Data may be easily transferred into other programs – e.g. a spreadsheet or word processing package

4 Accounting documents

Business organisations rely on relevant documentation to record the transactions that they undertake. Without an appropriate piece of supporting documentation, there is no way of knowing what has been bought, from whom and for how much, nor indeed what has been sold. With a high proportion of modern transactions being on credit, an accurate and comprehensive system of recording transactions is essential.

Many business documents are referred to as 'Primary Records'. They include:

* purchase orders
* delivery notes
* purchase invoices
* sales invoices
* debit notes
* credit notes

These documents are used to record business transactions in the first instance. For example, if an organisation wishes to purchase a new computer printer, it may first raise a purchase order which is sent to the supplier. The supplier would issue or deliver the printer along with a delivery note, to record the safe receipt of the goods. A supplier invoice requiring payment would follow. If the printer was faulty, it could be returned and a credit note issued.

In order for a transaction to be correctly recorded in a computerised accounting system, the appropriate documentation must first be raised and then the details entered into 'the system'; indeed, many organisations employ accounting staff whose job is primarily to enter the data accurately and completely from the source documents.

There are many other documents which are also essential in maintaining an up-to-date and accurate accounting system. Bank statements, schedules of direct debits/standing orders, supplier statements, correspondence from suppliers and customers and so on also provide invaluable information which can be used to check the computerised bookkeeping system for accuracy.

In the course of the case study which follows, you will be required to enter details from a range of source documents, and use other documents, to maintain a computerised bookkeeping system for a small company.

5 Retention of documents

There are legal requirements for businesses to retain source documents beyond the end of the accounting period to which they relate. The Limitations Act 1980 deals with this issue in general; however, there are many other pieces of specific legislation which place a responsibility on businesses to retain their records.

Accounting and Banking Records	
Ledgers, invoices, cheques, paying-in documents, bank statements and standing order instructions	Must all be retained for a minimum of six years
Employee Records	
All personnel records	6 years from end of employment
Senior Executive personnel records	Permanently
Rejected job applications	One year
Time cards, payroll records and expenses claims	Six years
Medical records and accident records	Permanently
Contractual Arrangements	
Simple contracts – e.g. with suppliers or customers	6 years after expiration of contract
Contracts relating to land and buildings	12 years after expiration of contract
Trust deeds (e.g. mortgages)	Permanently
Statutory Returns and Records of Board Meetings	
All statutory returns (e.g. to Companies House)	Permanently
Notices, circulars and minutes of board meetings	Permanently

Safe retention of records such as these is important not only to fulfil an organisation's legal obligations, but also because they may prove an invaluable source of reference – for example in a future complaint against a supplier.

However, all organisations must ensure that these documents are stored in such a way that they are easily accessible if required, kept secure from unauthorised access, and kept safe from physical damage (e.g. water or fire damage).

6 Coding

Most computerised bookkeeping systems work by the use of codes. Each supplier and each customer must be given a unique code by which the computer software can recognise them. It is vital that there can be no confusion between two suppliers with similar names. For example, you may be fully aware that John Green and John Greenwood are entirely different people, but it could be easy for a computer to mix them up. Each must therefore be given a unique code by which they can be identified.

Similarly, each product manufactured or sold by an organisation may be given a unique code. Employees, also, are usually 'coded' – you could check your pay slip to find your own Employee Reference Number.

Finally, every type of income or expense, asset or liability, is given a unique code to identify it. This makes entering transactions quite straightforward, since you need only refer to the relevant four digit code rather than a long narrative description.

Codes must be unique. However, they should also be recognisable by the person dealing with the system. For example, if a supplier was coded "SMITH006", this would be far more recognisable than a purely numeric code such as "0827329".

Care must be taken to issue codes that are not ambiguous. The use of a combination of letters and numbers (an alphanumeric code) often achieves this.

In SAGE, when you create a new customer or supplier record, the program will automatically suggest a code for that supplier. It does this by taking the first eight characters of the name. The suggested code for a customer called Greenwood would therefore be "GREENWOO". You may decide this is not the most appropriate code (think what the problem might be if you had two different suppliers called Greenwood), in which case you can easily change it. Many organisations have a set structure for coding, and if this is the case in your organisation you should follow it.

Installing SAGE for the first time

1 Installing SAGE

When you load SAGE v19 for the first time you should see the following screen:

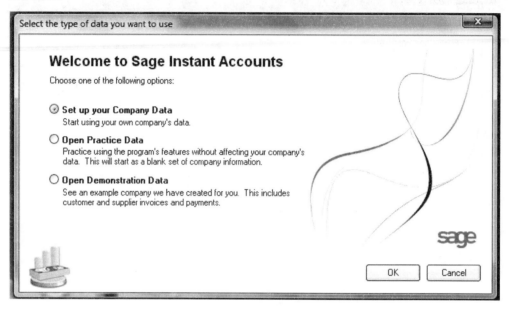

Assuming you are entering a new company, as you will be doing here, make sure that the "set up your company" option is marked. Don't worry at this stage about the other options – just press the [OK] button.

You should now see this screen:

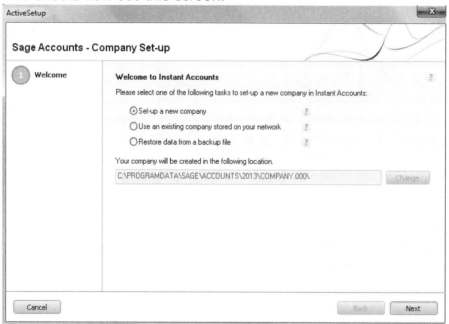

Your choice here depends on whether you are setting up a new company, or uploading existing data.

For now, you will be starting with a completely new company, so click on the "SET-UP A NEW COMPANY" button as shown.

Once you have company details set up and saved in SAGE, it will default to that company each time you start up.

KAPLAN PUBLISHING

Setting up your company

CONTENTS

1   Background to the company
2   Setting up the company

1 Background to the company

Wynn Bowlden is a self-employed tennis coach who operates as a sole trader. She coaches a range of clients from around the county of Mellinghamshire.

She rents a small office above a sports shop in the market town of Pickerton from which she conducts her business. As well as coaching her clients she also sells a range of tennis clothing and equipment which she obtains from a number of UK-based suppliers.

Wynn has asked you to help her with her bookkeeping. She currently uses a manual bookkeeping system. However, she now feels that the business has grown sufficiently to justify using a computerised accounting package, since she needs more timely and accurate financial information on which to base decisions about the business.

Today's date is 31st December 2013 – the last day of the business's financial year.

2 Setting up the company

Introduction

When you start using SAGE for your company you must firstly enter some information about the company itself. This is important because it will identify this particular company and appear on various reports. In addition, at this stage, you must enter the start dates of the company's financial year. This is vitally important, as SAGE will use this information in producing your annual accounts.

Data

You will need the following information for this session.

Business Name:	Wynn Bowlden Tennis Coach
Business Address:	15 Love Street
	Pickerton
	Mellinghamshire
	ML40 3TT
Telephone:	01989 2891891
Fax:	01989 2891891
Email:	info@wynnbowlden.webnet.uk
Website:	www.wynnbowlden.co.uk
VAT Number:	734 9281 07
Financial Year:	1st January – 31st December

Now we can begin entering the data for our business.

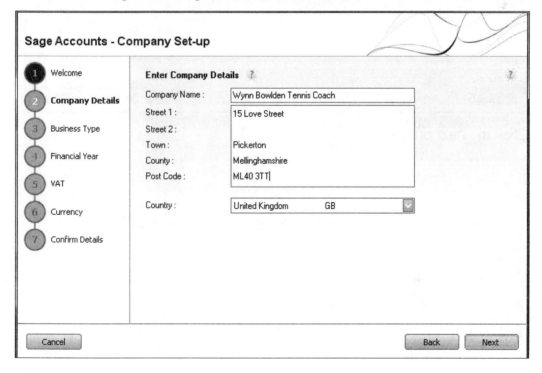

Be sure to check for accuracy – but don't worry if you make a mistake because you can always amend it later. Once you are happy with your entries click on the [Next] button.

Selecting the business type

On this screen you can choose a business type for your business: this amends the nominal codes so they are specific for your business. These are reference numbers by which we will refer to different types of asset, liability, income and expense as you start to enter transactions. You will learn more about nominal codes in Chapter 8. For this exercise we are going to select the Sole Trader type.

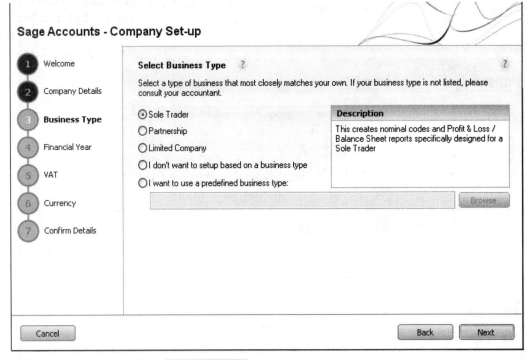

Click the next button [Next].

Entering the details of the Financial Year

This is a really important stage. You need to enter the dates of your company's Financial Year. Remember, for Wynn Bowlden the business's Financial Year is 1st January 2013 – 31st December 2013.

The data in this manual all refers to the year 2013, and so our Financial Year will start in **January 2013**. Enter this, using the drop down boxes.

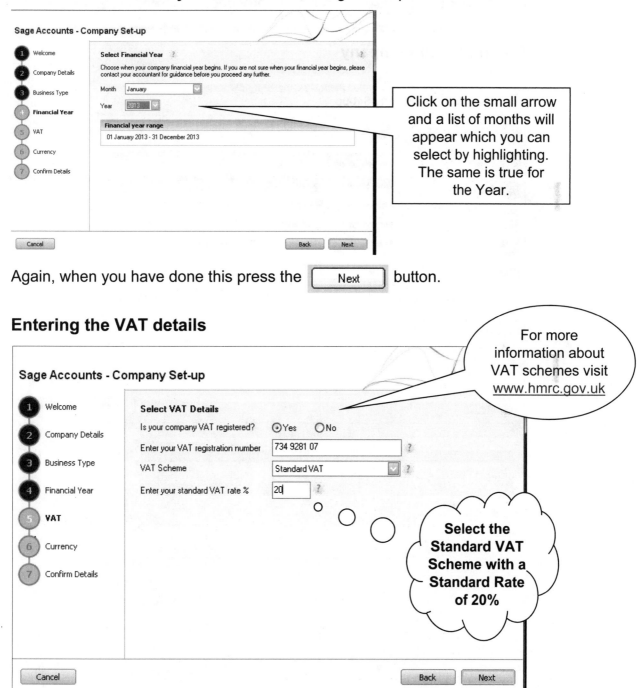

Again, when you have done this press the [Next] button.

Entering the VAT details

Entering the currency details

At this stage you can enter the currency details. All of Wynn Bowlden's transactions take place in the UK, and so their base currency is "Pound Sterling".

You should check that this option is correctly checked.

Again, click the [Next] button to proceed.

Creating your company

Active Setup

Well done – you have now set up SAGE with the basic information needed for the business. At this stage you can simply press the   Create   button to move to the next stage.

You will now be given information regarding how to obtain SAGE updates. Please read these carefully and proceed as you wish.

The first screen (or 'window') you will then see is shown below:

Take time to become familiar with the different options on this screen – you are unlikely to use all of them (at least to begin with), but it is good to explore them at this stage. When you are ready to move on to the next chapter, click on the   Customers   tab from the panel on the lower left hand side of the screen.

KAPLAN PUBLISHING

Navigating SAGE

CONTENTS

1 Introduction

You have by now opened your SAGE Instant software and set up the basic details of the business. The next stage is to check your business data and then to practise navigating your way around the different sections of SAGE. Don't worry if you have never used a package like SAGE before – so long as you can use a mouse you will be fine.

This 'window' (or screen) is the one that will now appear every time you open SAGE Instant. You will explore it in more detail as you progress through the manual. For now, just take the time to familiarise yourself with this screen. Make sure you maximise the screen.

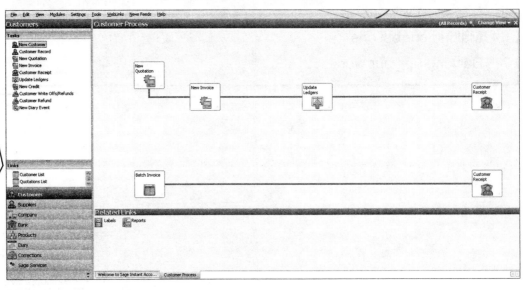

If you can't see the Links Panel simply place your cursor on the line and drag it upwards to expose the panel.

This screen enables you to access a range of accounting activities connected with your customers. You can:

1   Produce a new quotation for a potential customer.

2   Create an invoice to send or give to a customer.

3   Post (enter) the details of that invoice onto SAGE.

4   Receive and account for a payment made by a customer.

Note that you can access each of these activities in a number of ways.

The easiest are via:

(a)   The options on the *TASKS PANEL*

(b)   The options on the *LINKS PANEL*

(c)   The icons on the *CUSTOMER PROCESS* screen

You will practise each of these later on in this manual.

KAPLAN PUBLISHING

Of course, every business needs customers, but they are not the only aspect of a business. Any business will also need suppliers (of goods, raw materials and services). It will then also need to keep a record of the stock that it carries – whether of raw materials, work in progress or finished goods for sale. It will need a bank account (or maybe more than one!) in which to place its receipts and from which to make payments. SAGE also allows you to input accounting activities with each of these.

It is very simple to access the different parts of SAGE.

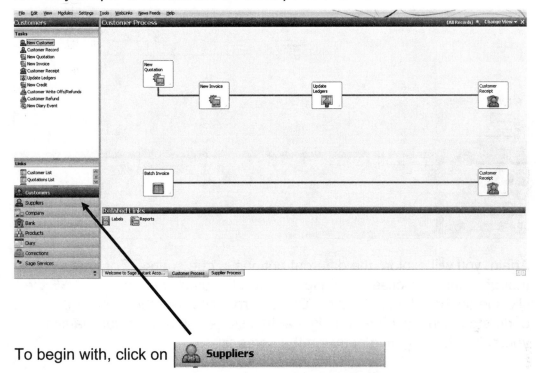

To begin with, click on   **Suppliers**

This will bring up a new window with a different series of icons.

2 The supplier process screen

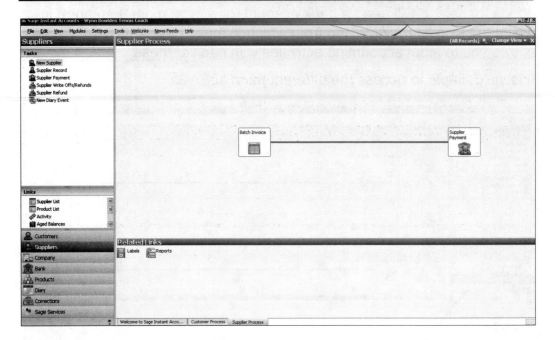

Again, you will explore the different options in due course. For now, though, simply practise switching between the different parts of SAGE by clicking on the relevant buttons. Don't worry about whether you can understand what you are seeing – at this stage you are just familiarising yourself with navigating between the screens.

Exercise

Start at the Customer Process Screen.

Navigate to the following screens:

❶   Suppliers ⇨ Supplier Payment (looks like 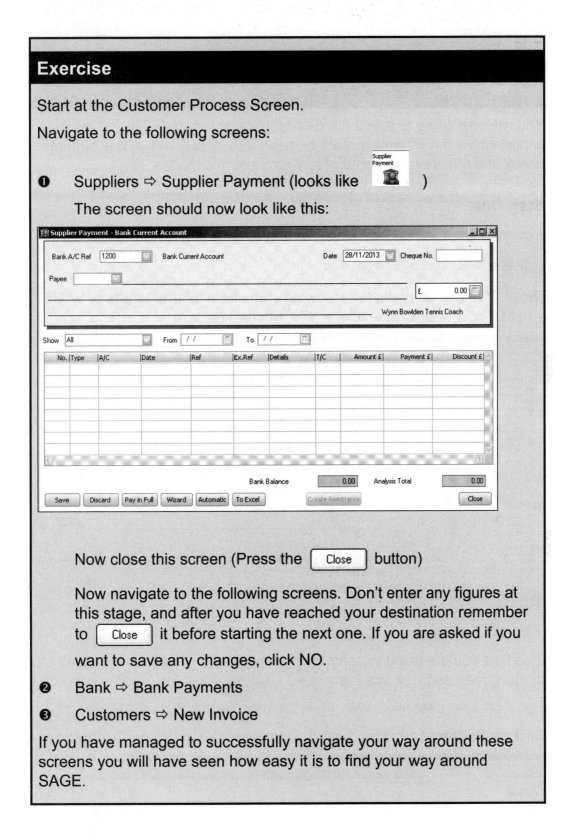   )

The screen should now look like this:

Now close this screen (Press the | Close | button)

Now navigate to the following screens. Don't enter any figures at this stage, and after you have reached your destination remember to | Close | it before starting the next one. If you are asked if you want to save any changes, click NO.

❷   Bank ⇨ Bank Payments

❸   Customers ⇨ New Invoice

If you have managed to successfully navigate your way around these screens you will have seen how easy it is to find your way around SAGE.

3 Checking your company details

You are now going to check the details that you entered earlier. This is important, as this information will be used throughout and so it is better to check and (if necessary) amend any errors at this stage.

Step One

Return to the 'Customer Process' screen by pressing

(**Note:** You can carry out the following steps from different parts of SAGE – but for now return to the 'Customer Process' screen)

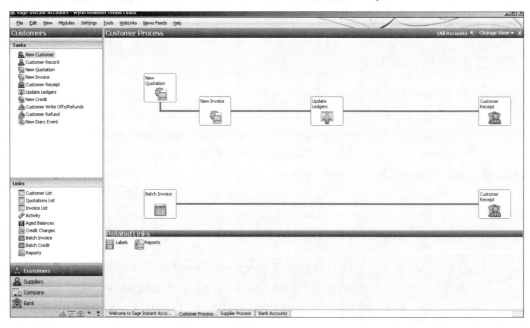

This time you are going to use the *drop down menus* that run along the top of the screen and look like this.

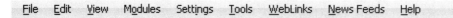

Click on **Settings,** and then from the menu select **Company Preferences.**

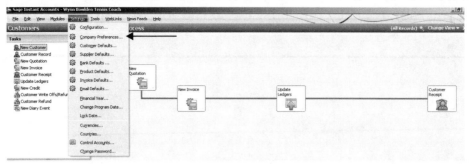

You will now be warned that all other sections of SAGE must be closed down before you can examine these company details. Make sure that you have done this and click the Yes button.

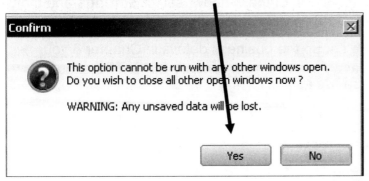

You should not have any data in any other sections at this point, and so you need not worry about losing it.

You will now see the company details that you input earlier. You should now thoroughly check these to make sure that they are correct.

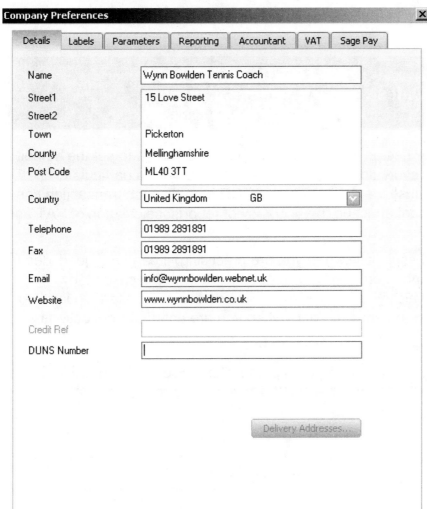

You can now check the information you entered about the financial year is also correct.

Again using the *menus* at the top of the window, select **Settings** and then **Financial Year.**

REMEMBER – when we set up the business details in Chapter 3 you entered the financial year as running from January 2013. This should now be showing on the screen, as below.

Make sure this is the correct date and then press OK. You will be asked to double-check this – again, confirm by pressing the Yes button.

4 Dates

Your computer has an internal clock, which SAGE uses to set the default date and time every time you open the package. This is particularly important because the date at which SAGE records each transaction can have a significant effect on the accuracy of reports, calculation of VAT and so on.

However (and especially when you are practising) it can be a good idea to override this and to enter your own date in line with the case study materials on which you are working. If you do this at the start, you will not need to keep re-entering the date when you are entering transactions.

To change the default program date

Imagine that you are working on a practice exercise, and you are told that today's date is 28th November 2013. However, the *real date* is 4th December 2013.

The default date in SAGE for entering transactions will show as 4th December – and you would have to override this each and every time you made an entry. This is repetitive and increases the likelihood of making a mistake – entering "05" instead of "04", for example.

Fortunately SAGE allows you to change the default date. Simply select the SETTINGS menu, and then CHANGE PROGRAM DATE.

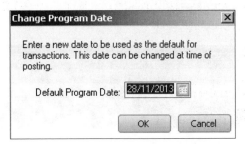

Now you can easily change the date that is required by the assessment material – in this particular case 28th November 2013. Now, every time you enter a transaction in SAGE the date will default to 28th November. This will have no effect on your computer's internal clock, and the next time you use the program the default date will revert to the real date once more until you change it.

Task

In the Wynn Bowlden Case Study, you are told that today's date is 31st December 2013. You should now change the SAGE program date on your computer to 31st December 2013. Remember that if you subsequently shut SAGE down, when you return to it you will need to change the default date again.

5 Checking your data

If you work steadily and carefully, you should not encounter many problems with your data entry. However, no matter how carefully you work, you will undoubtedly have to make corrections at some time – either because of human error in inputting data, or simply because new information comes to light.

One important feature of SAGE is the ability to check your data. This will help to identify any issues with data corruption (which can occur after a power cut, for example), missing data and date errors.

You can access the DataCheck facility by clicking on FILE in the main menu bar, then MAINTENANCE, and then CHECK DATA.

SAGE will check the validity of your data and advise you of any possible discrepancies.

You should note that the DataCheck facility will <u>not</u> identify data entry errors (e.g. entering the wrong amount or posting to the wrong nominal code). The accuracy of data entry is your responsibility, and you should therefore aim to minimise the number of errors you make by being careful to check your work at all stages.

6   Making corrections

Many people are understandably a little nervous when using a computer system for the first time. They worry that they may break the system, or make mistakes that cannot be corrected.

Don't worry: SAGE offers a number of easy ways to amend or wipe errors.

These are covered in more detail later, but for now let us look at one of the more common mistakes that you may make – the simple (but frustrating!) entry of an incorrect figure.

Example

Imagine you are entering a purchase of some stationery for £10.00. In error, you enter £100.00, and post the transaction into the system before you notice your mistake. What should you do?

To start with, don't panic!

One of the great advantages of a computerised system is that most errors are easy to correct. In SAGE, many amendments are carried out using the CORRECTIONS function.

This can be accessed by clicking on the Corrections option on the left hand side of the screen.

Alternatively, you can click on FILE in the main menu bar, then on MAINTENANCE, and finally CORRECTIONS.

You will now see a list of all the transactions you have entered in chronological order which can be amended

You now have two choices; you can either AMEND a previously-entered transaction, or DELETE it completely.

In the example above, you would simply want to amend the transaction. You could choose to amend the purchaser or supplier code, the product description, or the reference and date. In order to change other aspects of the transaction, such as the nominal code, the amounts or the VAT rate, you should click on the EDIT button.

It is relatively straightforward to correct most errors in this way; however, some errors require a different approach. These are covered in more detail later.

7 Backing up your work

It is important that you back up your data regularly, to guard against accidental losses which can prove very costly and time-consuming to recover or re-input.

Backing up your data should become part of your daily routine.

From the File menu at the top of the screen select 'Backup'.

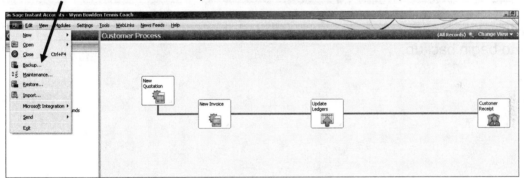

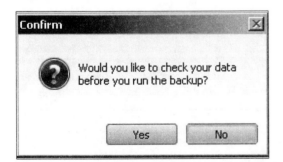

SAGE now asks if you would like to check your data before you run the backup – you should select [Yes]

Hopefully there are no problems with your data files and so you will now be able to backup your data.

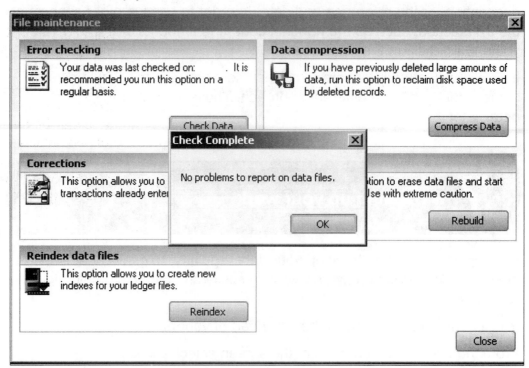

From this screen press the [OK] button, and then [Close] to begin backup.

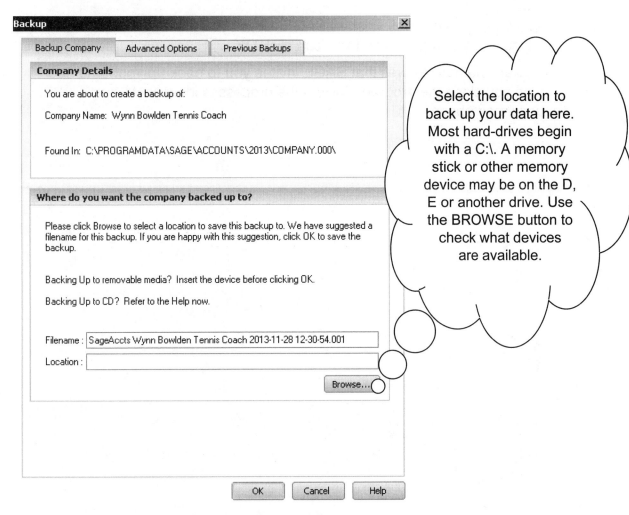

You need to select an appropriate file name – here, the name suggested by SAGE has been used but you could select another name to suit your own needs. Select **OK** to back up. The screen will now show a "Backup" box which indicates the progress of the backup.

When this process has finished SAGE will tell you that backup has been successfully completed and you can click **OK**.

You should note as well that SAGE invites you to back-up your data each time you close the program down – the process is identical to that described above.

Setting up your suppliers' details

5

CONTENTS

1 Introduction

Most business organisations will, over time, deal with a wide range of suppliers. A café may have different suppliers for their meat, cheese, vegetables, wine etc. A hairdresser will buy different products from different suppliers. Sometimes supplies will be obtained from a *wholesaler* or a *cash and carry*; other supplies may be sourced directly from the *manufacturers.*

The organisation will need to keep very accurate and timely records of all transactions with their suppliers. These transactions will typically include:

(1)   Purchases and returns

(2)   Discounts received from the supplier

(3)   Payments made to the supplier in settlement of outstanding bills

In addition, it would be very convenient to have all the contact details of every supplier easily to hand.

Fortunately SAGE provides a very comprehensive Supplier management system which covers all these requirements (and more). You will see how this works shortly, but firstly you will need to enter your suppliers' details.

2 Supplier data

Wynn Bowlden has five suppliers, whose details are given below:

Yonnad Tenniswear Ltd	**A/c Ref : YT001**

30 Sampras Lane
Laver
Derbyshire
DB18 8HY

Tel 01829 389228

Contact: Holly Maclay

Outstanding Balance at 31st December 2013: **£864.10**

Credit Terms: **30 days, 2% 7 days**   **Credit Limit £2,500**

Kike Shoes Ltd	**A/c Ref : KS001**

40 Murray Street
Rosewall
North Yorkshire
YO18 8DV

Tel 0845 2381989

Contact: Emily WIlls

Outstanding Balance at 31st December 2013: **£1,208.19**

Credit Terms: **30 days, 2% 7 days**   **Credit Limit £2,500**

Wilkinson Tennis Balls Ltd	**A/c Ref : WT003**

30 Blake Avenue
Great Ashe
Somerset
SM18 6FG

Tel 0800 3898191

Contact: Emma Moore

Outstanding Balance at 31st December 2013: **£1529.10**

Credit Terms: **14 days, no settlement discount**   **Credit Limit £3,000**

Wotta Rackets Ltd   A/c Ref : WR002
30 Nadal Way
Little Evert
Edinburgh
ED17 3HP

Tel 0800 1902029

Contact: Ruby Catt

Outstanding Balance at 31st December 2013: **£209.34**

Credit Terms: **21 days, 1% 7 days**   **Credit Limit £1,000**

First Serve Office Supplies Ltd   A/c Ref : FS001
15 Venus Heights
Mottram
Devon
SW88 7BV

Tel 0845 8728382

Contact: Robin Holly

Outstanding Balance at 31st December 2013: **£401.35**

Credit Terms: **30 days, 2.5% 10 days**   **Credit Limit £2,500**

3 Entering supplier details

From the Supplier Process window (below) press the **New Supplier** task.

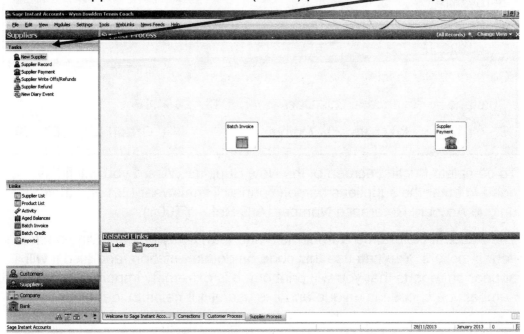

This will bring up the Supplier Record Wizard, which will help you to easily enter your suppliers' details.

To continue with this you will need to refer to the list of suppliers for Wynn Bowlden on the previous pages.

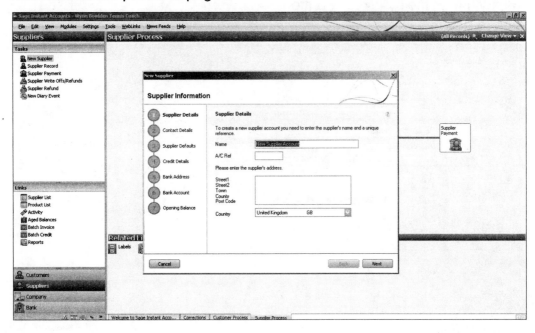

The first supplier to enter is:

Yonnad Tenniswear Ltd	**A/c Ref : YT001**

Yonnad Tenniswear Ltd
30 Sampras Lane
Laver
Derbyshire
DB18 8HY

Tel 01829 389228

Contact: Holly Maclay

Outstanding Balance at 31st December 2013: **£864.10**

Credit Terms: **30 days, 2% 7 days**   **Credit Limit £2,500**

To complete the first screen of the New Supplier Wizard you will firstly need to enter the supplier's name (Yonnad Tenniswear Ltd) and their unique Account Reference Number (A/C Ref – YT001).

The Account Reference Number is a shorthand way of identifying each of your suppliers. You can use this code on documentation, and also it will appear on reports that you will print out. It is extremely important that the number you choose is unique and it is useful if it helps to identify the supplier in some way – here YT001 is representing **Y**onnad **T**enniswear.

It is important to check your spelling for accuracy as errors (although they can be rectified) can cause confusion. In particular, ensure you use the correct account code (YT001) as this *cannot* subsequently be changed.

You will then need to enter the supplier's address. Again, when you are happy, press the [Next] button.

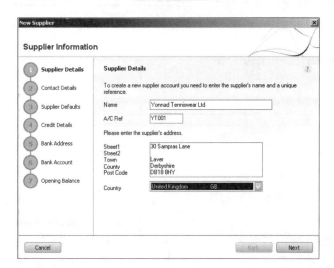

KAPLAN PUBLISHING

Now you can enter the firm's contact details. In this case we have not got an e-mail or website address, or the VAT number. Don't worry, though, as these can easily be entered at a later date. You can enter Holly Maclay's name at this point, though, before pressing the [Next] button.

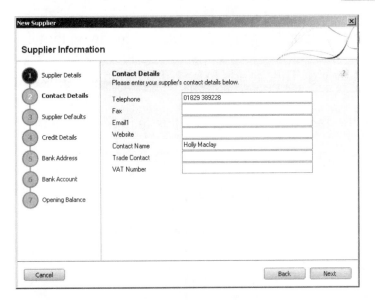

On the next screen, we can check the supplier default details. The nominal code in which transactions with this supplier will be recorded is 5000 (you will learn more about nominal codes later) and the VAT code is T1, meaning that the majority of purchases from this supplier will have VAT added at 20.0%.

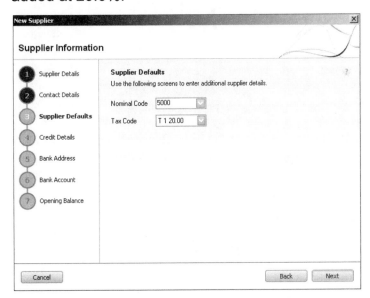

The next screen asks you to enter details of your credit terms with this supplier. Here we can enter the credit limit of £2500. If you are happy with this press the button.

You can also enter details of any credit terms that the supplier offers. Most suppliers will insist on payment within a certain period of time – typically seven to twenty eight days **(the payment days).** However, some suppliers may also offer a discount for payment within an earlier period **(the settlement days)**.

Yonnad Tenniswear Ltd offer credit terms of **"2% 7days"** meaning that if Wynn Bowlden settles invoices within 7 days she can deduct a 2% discount from the amount owing. This needs to be reflected in the window as shown below.

You will also want to tick the terms agreed box, as this tells Sage that the details have been confirmed.

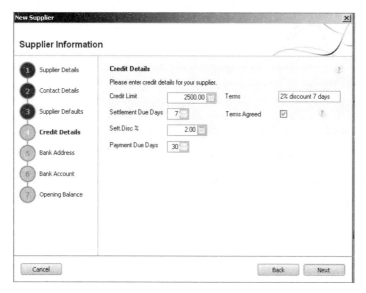

The next screens ask you to enter the details of your supplier's bank. This is essential if you will be paying the supplier using methods such as BACS. It is not necessary if you will always be paying by cheque. You can leave these blank for this example as you have not been given the information to complete these.

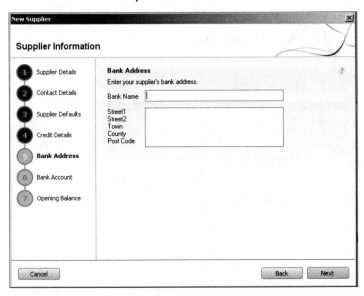

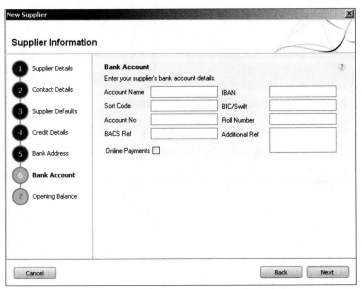

SAGE now asks if this supplier has an outstanding balance – in other words, if at the time of entering their details you already owe them money. In this example, Wynn Bowlden currently owes Yonnad Tenniswear Ltd £864.10. This figure can be entered either as one figure, or alternatively could be entered as a series of figures representing each of the different outstanding invoices at the time of entry.

For now, you should choose to enter the outstanding balance as one figure.

Remember today's date is 31st December 2013. This is therefore the date on which we will be entering our opening balances. On the following screen either type the date (31/12/2013) or use SAGE's calendar facility to enter it. Of course, if you changed the SAGE default date earlier this will be the date automatically displayed for you!

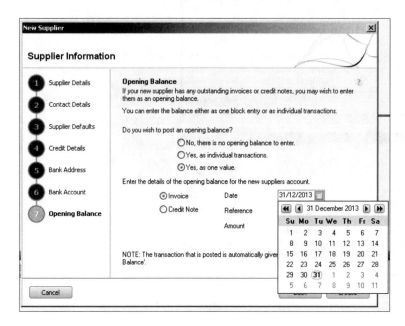

You can now enter the opening balance for Yonnad Tenniswear Ltd. Check your entries then press the [Next] button.

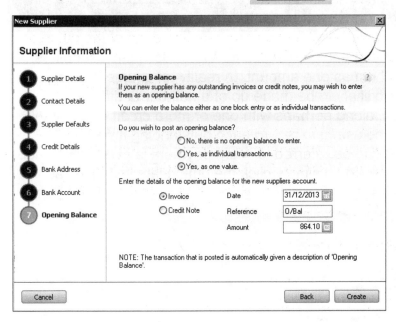

Well done! You have now entered your first supplier details. To recap, you began by entering their company details, such as their address, phone and fax numbers and contact details. Then you entered the credit terms that this supplier makes available to us, including normal payment terms and any discounts that are available for early settlement.

After that you entered your supplier's bank details and finally the opening balance of debt to that supplier.

SAGE now confirms that you have successfully entered the supplier's details.

The next stage is important – you *must* press the [Create] button to save the details and to post the opening balance.

Exercise

Refer back to section 2 of this chapter. You have already entered one of Wynn Bowlden's suppliers (Yonnad Tenniswear Ltd).

You should now enter the full details for each of the remaining suppliers, and then save them to SAGE.

4 Entering detailed invoices or nil balances

When you entered the opening balances for Wynn Bowlden's suppliers, you simply entered them as one amount. In reality, of course, these opening balances are likely to be made up of a number of different outstanding invoices, along perhaps with one or more credit notes. If this is the case, it would be useful to record each outstanding invoice separately, so that it can be referred to when payment is eventually made. In order to do this, you would simply click the button labelled "Yes, as individual transactions".

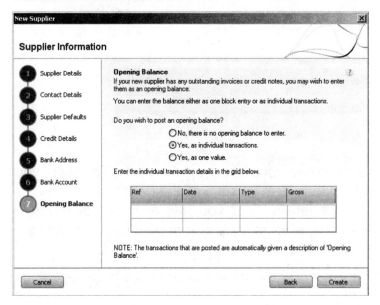

You will now be able to enter each outstanding invoice or credit note individually.

Entering Zero Balances

Sometimes an existing supplier will have no outstanding invoices at the date they are entered into the system. In this situation, simply click on the "No, there is no opening balance to enter" button.

5 Printing supplier data reports

You have entered the details of the five suppliers, so let's now check that they are correct by running off a report from SAGE. Printing reports in SAGE is straightforward, using the Report Browser Function.

Firstly, select Suppliers, and then choose Supplier List from the Links section down the left-hand side of the screen. This presents all the suppliers that you have entered so far in a list format, as shown below, including their outstanding balances.

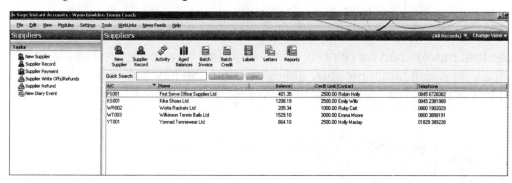

Now select the **Reports** icon from the ribbon at the top of the screen or from the Links menu in the left-hand pane on the screen. This will open a new window with a list of supplier-related reports that you could want to print and use. Reports you access regularly can be designated as "favourites" by clicking on the star icon next to the report name.

You will practise accessing some more of these later on, but for now the one that you want is the report entitled *Supplier Address List* within *the Suppliers details* option. To access the contents of this (or any) folder simply click on it.

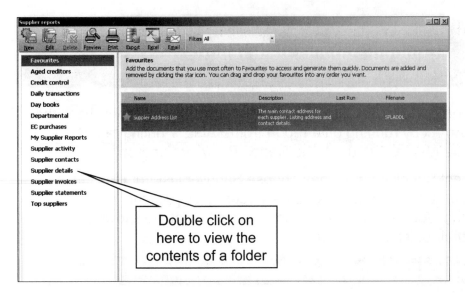

Double click on
here to view the
contents of a folder

Note that reports can be printed, previewed (on screen), saved to file or
sent as an email attachment by selecting from the icons displayed when
you hover next to the report name in the Report Browser.

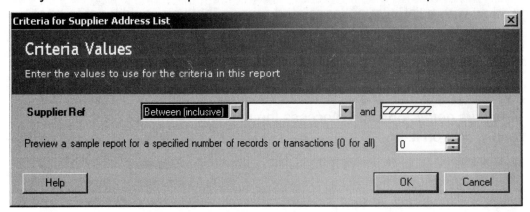

On the next screen you can identify the criteria by which you wish to select
the contents of your report. As you wish to see a list of all the suppliers
that you have entered keep the boxes as shown below, then press OK.

Your report should now show on screen, similar to the one below.

Date:	28/11/2013	**Wynn Bowlden Tennis Coach**			Page: 1
Time:	13:51:24	**Supplier Address List**			

Supplier From:
Supplier To: ZZZZZZZZ

A/C	Name	Contact	Telephone	Fax
FS001	First Serve Office Supplies Ltd 15 Venus Heights Mottram Devon SW88 7BV	Robin Holly	0845 8728382	
KS001	Kike Shoes Ltd 40 Murray Street Rosewall North Yorkshire YO18 8DV	Emily Wills	0845 2381989	
WR002	Wotta Rackets Ltd 30 Nadal Way Little Evert Edingburgh ED17 3HP	Ruby Catt	0800 1902029	
WT003	Wilkinson Tennis Balls Ltd 30 Blake Avenue Great Ashe Somerset SM18 6FG	Emma Moore	0800 3898191	
YT001	Yonnad Tenniswear Ltd 30 Sampras Lane Laver Derbyshire DB18 8HY	Holly Maclay	01829 389228	

There are many other supplier reports available in this section – you should now feel confident enough to access these and to print them out. The exact list of reports that you will use will depend on your particular requirements, and you will see some of the more common ones later in this manual.

Setting up your customers' details

CONTENTS

1 Introduction

Now that you have successfully entered your suppliers' details you can now move on to enter relevant information about your customers as well.

The process of entering your customers' details is very similar to that of entering supplier information, so you should feel confident doing this now.

It is of course vitally important that you keep accurate records for each of your customers. This information is likely to include:

(1)   Sales made on credit to customers, and sales returns

(2)   Credit terms for your customers, including any discount they may receive

(3)   Contact details for easy invoicing

(4)   Payments received from customers

Consistent, accurate recording of information is a vital aspect of any credit management system, ensuring that your organisation gets paid as quickly as possible for its sales. This can be the difference between failure and survival for most businesses.

2   Customer data

Wynn Bowlden has five customers with outstanding balances as at 31st December 2013. Their details are given below:

Roland Garros	**A/c Ref : GAR001**
10 Paris Boulevard	
Hostleton	
Mellinghamshire	
HO97 6TF	

Outstanding Balance at 31st December 2013: **£301.28**

Credit Terms: **Payment in 28 days**   **Credit Limit £500**

Rank Outsiders Ltd	**A/c Ref : RAN002**
No2 Court Trading Estate	
Tarryton	
Mellinghamshire	
TY17 6DS	

Outstanding Balance at 31st December 2013: **£1820.49**

Credit Terms: **Payment in 28 days**   **Credit Limit £5000**

Noah Chang	**A/c Ref : CHA001**
40 Love Street	
Portshead	
Mellinghamshire	
PH28 5CV	

Outstanding Balance at 31st December 2013: **£109.26**

Credit Terms: **Payment in 28 days**   **Credit Limit £500**

Little Smashers Junior Tennis Club   A/c Ref : LIT001
No 1 Sinceperry Avenue
Hurby
Mellinghamshire
HB80 9PL

Outstanding Balance at 31st December 2013: **£209.47**

Credit Terms: **Payment in 28 days**   **Credit Limit £1000**

Annette Chord   A/c Ref : CHO001
20 New York Street
Bridgeford
Mellinghamshire
BG16 9JY

Outstanding Balance at 31st December 2013: **£819.20**

Credit Terms: **Payment in 28 days**   **Credit Limit £1000**

You will now enter these five customer details into SAGE.

Step One

Go to the Customer Process screen, as below.

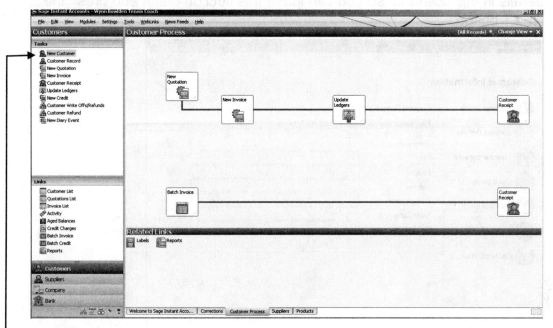

From the Task Bar, click on New Customer. You should now be able to enter your first customer's details, as below.

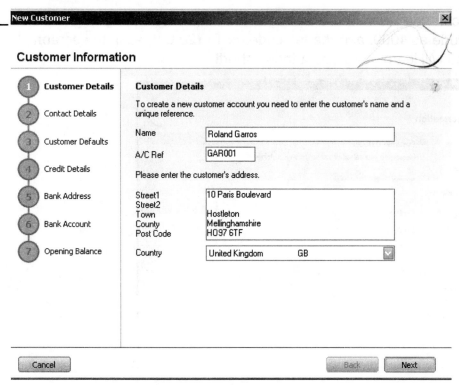

When you have done this click the NEXT button again, and enter the contact details for the customer. You aren't given any customer contact details in this scenario, so you can leave this section blank and press the NEXT button.

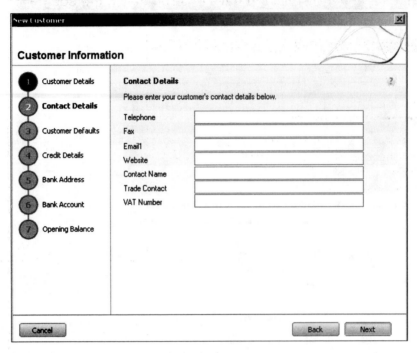

Now you can now view the default details for this customer. Leave the nominal code as 4000, and the tax code as T1 (20.00), as in the screen below. You will learn more about these shortly

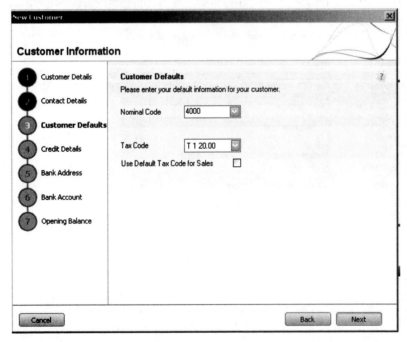

Now you can enter the credit terms. For Mr Garros we will require payment within 28 days, and there is no settlement discount for early payment. Be careful to enter all information accurately and correctly at every stage of this process – check that the details you have entered match the source data.

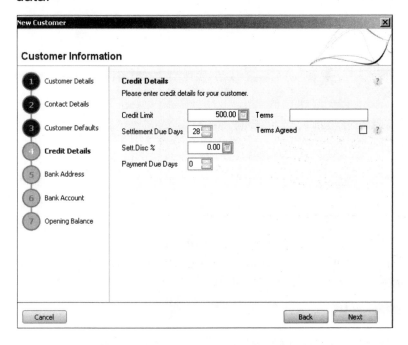

SAGE will now give you the option of entering the bank details for your customers. As with the supplier process earlier, you can leave these blank as you are not given the information to complete them for this case study.

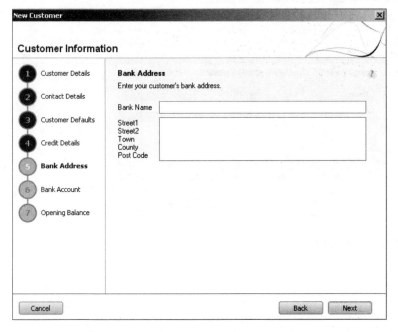

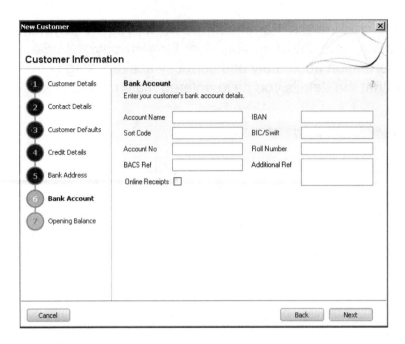

SAGE will now ask if there are any opening balances, and as with the supplier entry screen you can enter these in one of three ways. Again, you should choose to enter them as a single value.

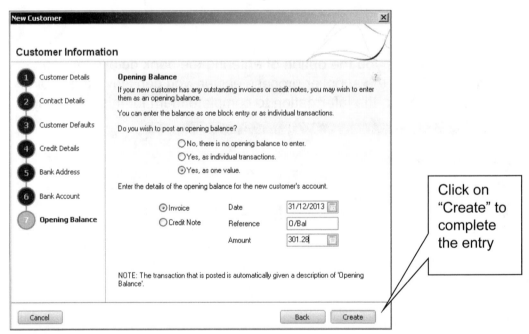

Click on "Create" to complete the entry

Enter the opening balance for Mr Garros (£301.28) as above.

Activity

Refer back to section 2 of this chapter. You have already entered one of Wynn Bowlden's customers (Mr Roland Garros).

You should now enter the full details for each of the remaining customers, and then save them to SAGE. When you have done this your screen should look like this:

Remember – you may need to Change View to 'Customers' to see the list like this – just as you did for Suppliers in Chapter 5.

3 Printing customer data reports

You have entered the details of the five customers, so let's now check that they are correct by running off a report from SAGE.

The first report to print is the Customer List. The Report Browser for Customers works in the same way as for Suppliers – refer to Chapter 5 to remind yourself of this.

From the **Customers** window, click on **Reports** to open the Report Browser.

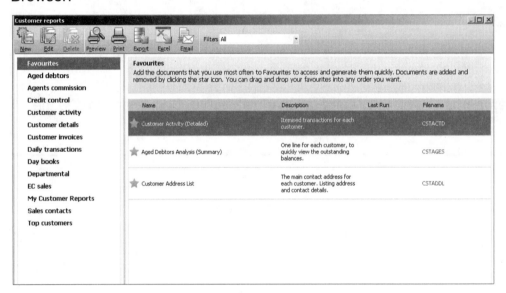

This will produce a new window with a list of customer-related reports that you could want to print and use. You will practise accessing some more of these later on, but for now the one that you want is the report entitled *Customer Address List*. This is contained within the folder called *Customer Details* – to access the contents of this (or any) folder simply double-click on it.

Double click on *Customer Address List* to produce the report.

On the next screen you can identify the criteria by which you wish to select the contents of your report. As you wish to see a list of all the customers that you have entered keep the boxes as shown overleaf, then press OK.

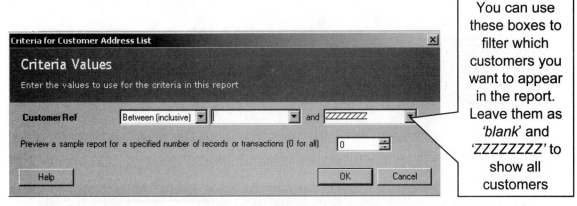

You can use these boxes to filter which customers you want to appear in the report. Leave them as *'blank'* and *'ZZZZZZZZ'* to show all customers

Your report should now show on screen, similar to the one below.

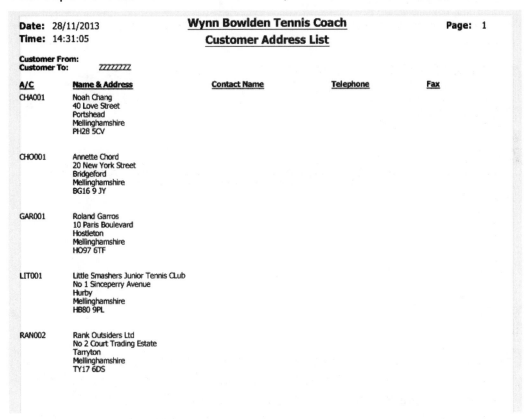

There are many other supplier reports available in this section – you should now feel confident enough to access these and to print them out. The exact list of reports that you will use will depend on your particular requirements, and you will see some of the more common ones later in this manual.

Product lines for sale

7

CONTENTS

1 Introduction
2 Product categories
3 Products

1   Introduction

SAGE allows you to differentiate between sales of different types of products. You will need to open the Configuration option in the Settings tab along the top of the screen.

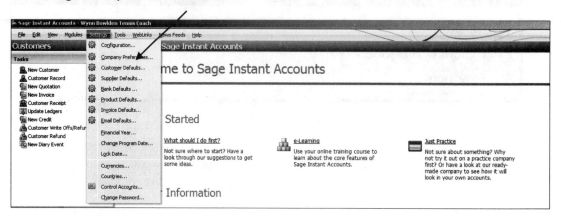

The screen that appears, shown below, is then used to set the defaults. You will need to make sure you have selected the Products tab along the top of this screen.

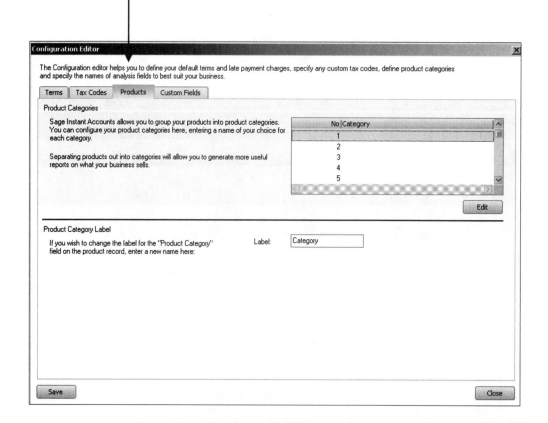

2 Product categories

You are going to set up five different product categories, as follows:

(1) Tennis Racquets

(2) Tennis Balls

(3) Clothing – Men

(4) Clothing – Women

(5) Footwear

SAGE Instant v.19 will allow you to enter up to 999 different categories of product – but these five will suffice for now!

To amend a product category, use your cursor to highlight the number with a blue bar, and then click [Edit]. You can then easily type in your new description.

You should now set up the five product categories for Wynn Bowlden, as outlined above.

Your screen should now look like the one below.

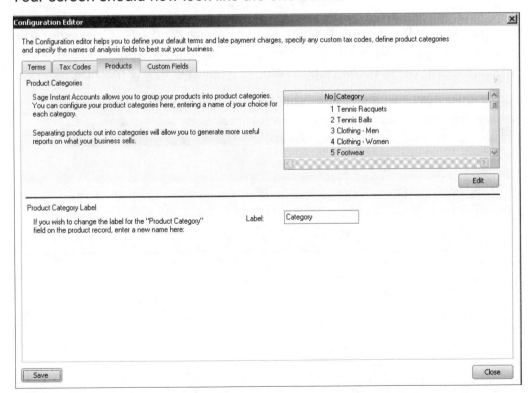

You should now click on the [Save] button and save the changes.

You can of course add new product categories at any time.

3 Products

In order to set up different product lines, select **MODULES – PRODUCTS – NEW PRODUCT.** This launches the New Product Wizard, which requires you to enter a Product Description and a unique Product Code, as well as other relevant information. For now, you are going to enter just three products, each of which is a tennis racquet. These are:

Name	Code	Location	Selling Price	Sales Code	Supplier	Cost Price
Bazooka	BAZ1	Shop	£80.00	4000	Wotta Rackets Ltd	£30.00
Turbo	TUR1	Shop	£100.00	4000	Wotta Rackets Ltd	£40.00
Maxi	MAX1	Shop	£150.00	4000	Wotta Rackets Ltd	£70.00

You should use the wizard to enter each of these products. Only enter the information given above – for now, you can leave boxes such as the IntraStat Com. Code blank (these refer to trading with EU members)

You should now see the following screen showing your product lines.

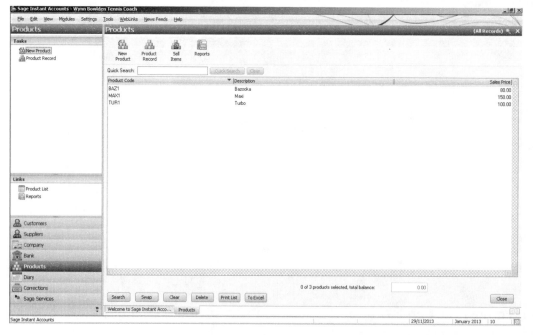

The nominal ledger

CONTENTS

1 Introduction

The nominal ledger is probably the most important element of the SAGE (or indeed any) accounting system. This is simply a series of different accounts into which money is debited or credited each time a transaction is recorded.

Each of these accounts is given a unique four digit code number. To view the list of Nominal Codes go to the COMPANY screen, and then NOMINAL LEDGER.

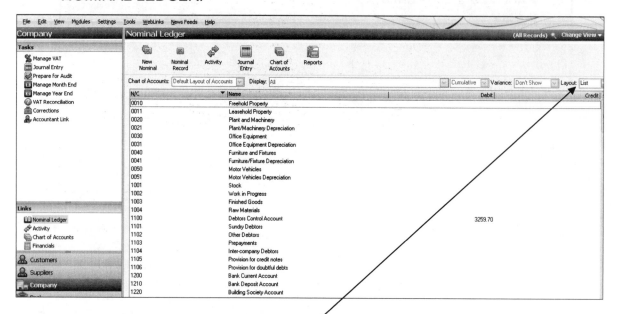

Select **'List'** from the layout menu.

This now shows you a list of all of the nominal codes (N/Cs) for the business.

The four-digit code is important, as the list is actually broken down into groups:

0000-0999	Fixed Assets and Depreciation (e.g. Buildings, Equipment)
1000-1999	Current Assets (e.g. Stock, Debtors, Bank)
2000-2299	Short Term Liabilities (e.g. Creditors)
2300-2999	Long Term Liabilities (e.g. Loans)
3000-3999	Capital and Reserves
4000-4999	Sales
5000-5999	Purchases
6000-6999	Direct Expenses (e.g. Direct Labour)
7000-7999	Miscellaneous Overheads (e.g. Phone, Rent, Postage)
8000-8999	Bad debts and Depreciation
9000-9999	Suspense and Mispostings

SAGE uses these 'groupings' of codes to ensure that items appear in the correct part of the Profit and Loss Account or Balance Sheet. You can easily amend the description of a nominal code, or indeed add a new one, but you must always make sure that you keep the code in the correct 'grouping' for the type of account that it is.

You should now print out the list of nominal codes. Do this by simply pressing the Print List button.

The full list of default Nominal Codes should now print, taking approximately three pages.

You should now keep this list safe, as you will need to use it when entering transactions in the future.

Control Accounts

There are some very special Nominal Codes called Control Accounts, which are essential to the running of the SAGE software. These cannot be deleted and are always present in the Chart of Accounts. To view them go to SETTINGS (in the tabs at the top of the screen) – CONTROL ACCOUNTS. This will show you the main Control Accounts within SAGE, as shown below.

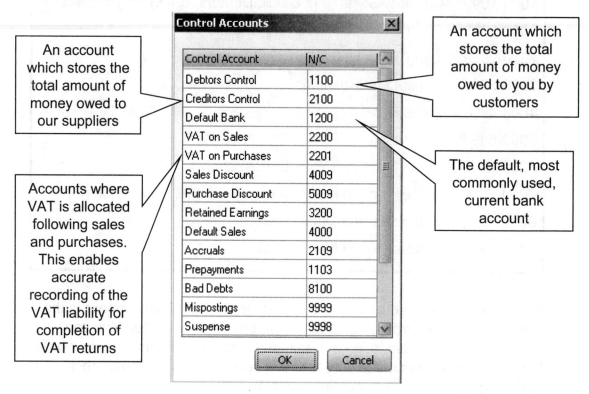

An account which stores the total amount of money owed to our suppliers

An account which stores the total amount of money owed to you by customers

Accounts where VAT is allocated following sales and purchases. This enables accurate recording of the VAT liability for completion of VAT returns

The default, most commonly used, current bank account

Most of these accounts are used automatically by SAGE. This means that you do not need to specify them individually when entering transactions – SAGE will work out which control account is required and apply it automatically. Other Nominal Codes (from the list you printed out) will need to be entered.

2 Entering a nominal code

The default Chart of Accounts contains the most common codes set up for a general business. However, you will almost certainly want to add to, or amend, these Nominal Codes to suit your business in particular.

For example, Wynn Bowlden will want to be more specific when recording her sales and purchases. Have a look at your listing of Nominal Codes. Find the 5000-5999 Range (remember, these are set aside for Purchases).

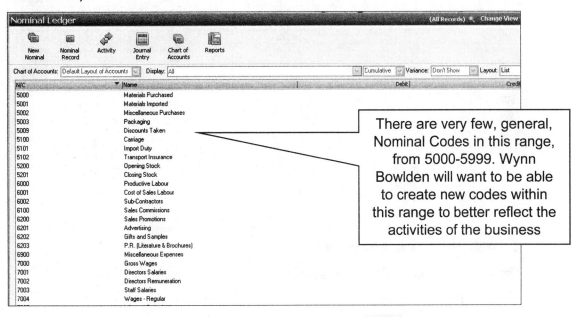

There are very few, general, Nominal Codes in this range, from 5000-5999. Wynn Bowlden will want to be able to create new codes within this range to better reflect the activities of the business

Now, from within the NOMINAL module click on the Nominal Record button.

You should now have a blank record screen, as below.

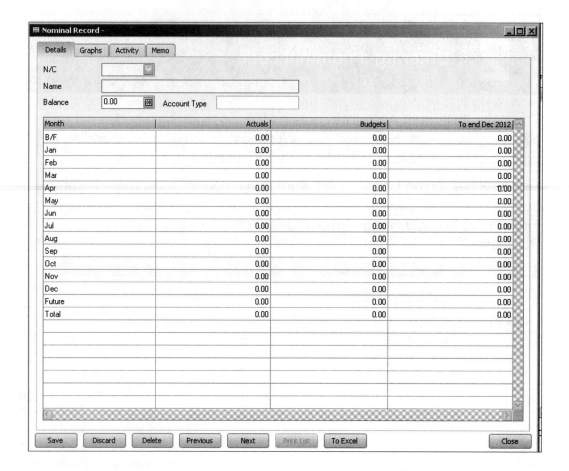

To **AMEND** an existing code:

Enter the Nominal Code (or select from the pull down menu)

Type in the new name

To **CREATE** a new code:

Enter the new Nominal Code (making sure it is in the correct range)

Type in the new name

Exercise

To practice amending and creating Nominal Codes, enter each of the following N/Cs and names. Do them one by one, and then save each one.

SALES		PURCHASES	
Nominal Code	*Name*	*Nominal Code*	*Name*
4000	Sales –Equipment	5000	Purchases – Equipment
4001	Sales – Clothing and Footwear	5001	Purchases – Clothing and Footwear
4002	Sales – Individual Coaching	5002	Purchases – Stationery
4003	Sales – Group Coaching	5003	Purchases – Packaging
4004	Sales – Other	5004	Purchases – Other Consumables

Once you have entered these, close down the window and generate the Nominal List report for the range 4000-5999. You do this by using the Report Browser as before, but this time within the Company, Nominal ledger section of SAGE. You will find the Nominal List Report in the folder named **Nominal Details.**

To select the range 4000-5999, use the Criteria Values screen:

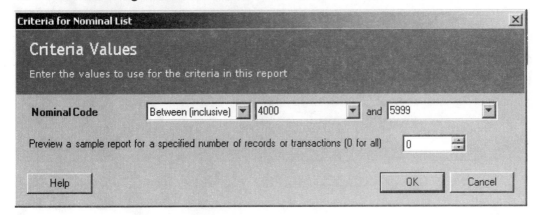

The report should look like this:

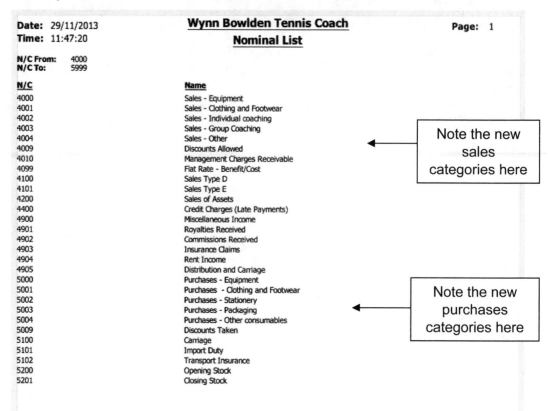

Date: 29/11/2013	Wynn Bowlden Tennis Coach	Page: 1
Time: 11:47:20	Nominal List	

N/C From: 4000
N/C To: 5999

N/C	Name
4000	Sales - Equipment
4001	Sales - Clothing and Footwear
4002	Sales - Individual coaching
4003	Sales - Group Coaching
4004	Sales - Other
4009	Discounts Allowed
4010	Management Charges Receivable
4099	Flat Rate - Benefit/Cost
4100	Sales Type D
4101	Sales Type E
4200	Sales of Assets
4400	Credit Charges (Late Payments)
4900	Miscellaneous Income
4901	Royalties Received
4902	Commissions Received
4903	Insurance Claims
4904	Rent Income
4905	Distribution and Carriage
5000	Purchases - Equipment
5001	Purchases - Clothing and Footwear
5002	Purchases - Stationery
5003	Purchases - Packaging
5004	Purchases - Other consumables
5009	Discounts Taken
5100	Carriage
5101	Import Duty
5102	Transport Insurance
5200	Opening Stock
5201	Closing Stock

Note the new sales categories here

Note the new purchases categories here

Well done! Now you can amend or create new nominal codes. The next step is to post opening balances to each relevant nominal code within SAGE for your business. This means that you will be entering the financial balance on each account for Wynn Bowlden, as at the first date you begin using the SAGE system to record financial transactions for the company. Remember for Wynn Bowlden this was 31st December 2013. The list of opening balances is shown below:

Wynn Bowlden

Opening Balances

	Nominal code	Debit	Credit
Motor vehicles (at cost)	0050	8000.00	
Depreciation (Motor Vehicles)	0051		2000.00
Office Equipment	0030	3420.00	
Depreciation (Office Equipment)	0031		1710.00
Stock (as at 1st January 2013)	1001	2865.90	
Debtors Control Account	1100	3259.70	
Petty Cash	1230	100.00	
Bank	1200	12416.60	
Creditors Control Account	2100		4212.08
VAT Liability	2202		981.61
Capital	3000		3500.00
Profit and Loss Account	3200		4121.14
Sales – Equipment	4000		2016.53
Sales – Clothing and Footwear	4001		2195.46
Sales – Individual Coaching	4002		13229.30
Sales – Group Coaching	4003		13450.50
Sales – Other	4004		601.60
Purchases – Equipment	5000	1015.20	
Purchases – Clothing and Footwear	5001	1310.60	
Purchases – Stationery	5002	415.20	
Purchases – Packaging	5003	208.78	
Purchases – Other Consumables	5004	104.61	
Rent	7100	3600.00	
General Rates	7103	350.00	
Telephone	7550	491.52	
Miscellaneous Motor Expenses	7304	8604.47	
General expenses	8207	1855.64	
		48018.22	**48018.22**

Note: This is the total of the suppliers' balances that you entered earlier. This has already been entered and so will not need to be entered again.

Similarly this is the total of the individual customers' accounts that you entered earlier. Again, this will not need to be entered again.

Entering a new balance

Entering opening balances in SAGE is very straightforward.

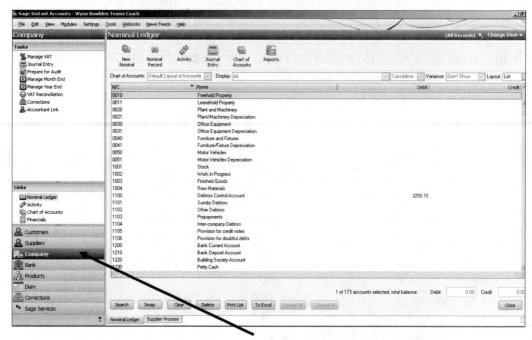

From the main screen click on the  button.

Highlight the Nominal Code for which you want to enter an opening balance.

The first amount we need to enter is for Motor Vehicles – the amount is £8,000. This is a **debit balance**, because it represents the cost of the motor vehicles (a fixed asset) owned by the business. You can see that Motor Vehicles has been automatically assigned a Nominal Code of **0050** by SAGE.

Double-click your mouse on this code.

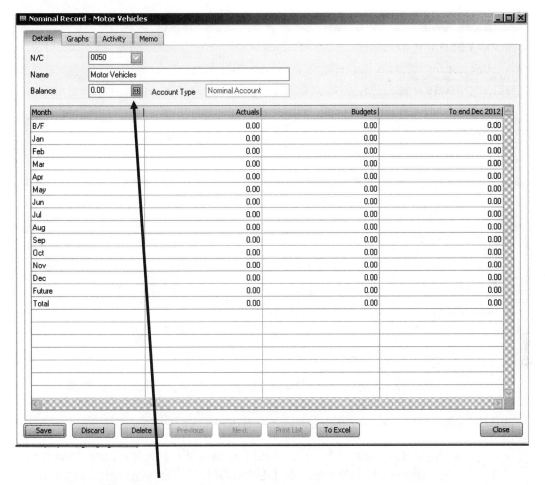

Now click on the 'Opening Balance' icon.

Keep the Ref as "O/Bal". Change the date box to 31st December 2013 if necessary and enter the opening balance amount of £8,000.00 in the Debit box. Leave the credit box at zero. Then click the Save button.

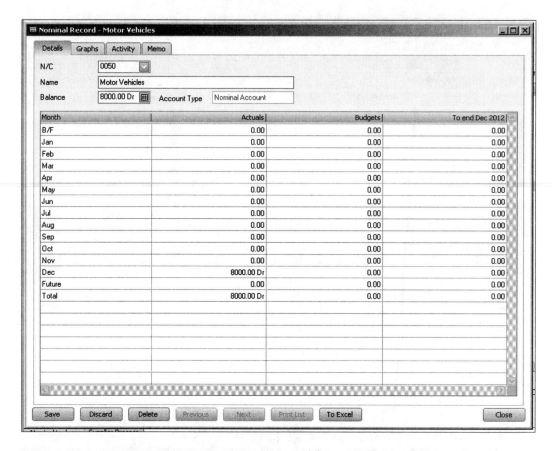

Notice how the detail record for Nominal Code 0050 (Motor Vehicles) has now changed, showing your entry in December. When you return to the Nominal Ledger page you should also see the new balance reflected there.

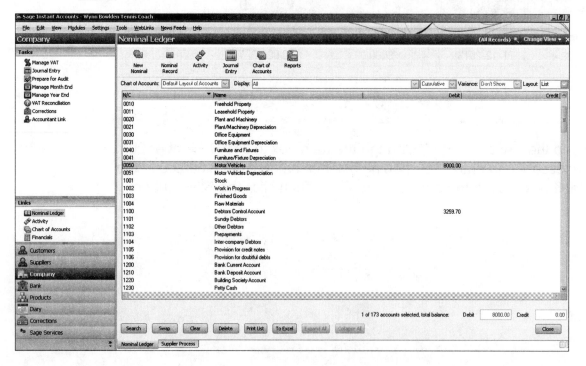

Exercise

You should now be able to enter the opening balances for each of the accounts.

Important

1   You will need to create a new Nominal Code for the balance for General Expenses (use code 8207), and amend the name of the account for code 7550 to "Telephone"

2   You do not need to enter opening balances for two items, the Debtors Control Account and the Creditors Control Account. This is because these represent the total amount owed to us (debtors) and the total amount we owe (creditors), made up of all of the individual balances you entered earlier. These control account balances are therefore calculated automatically by SAGE and you do not enter them.

3   Be careful to enter each balance correctly as either a **debit** or a **credit** balance.

3 Printing a trial balance

You have now entered all the opening balances for Wynn Bowlden. You are now ready to begin entering transactions on a day to day basis. Before that though, you should print off a Trial Balance.

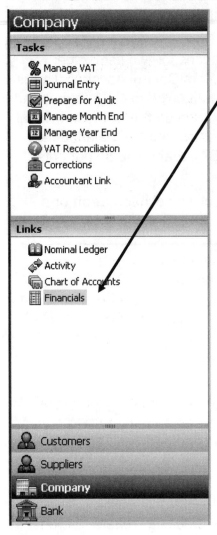

From the Company screen, select Financials in the links section.

This will create a new screen, from which you can quickly produce a series of the most useful reports in SAGE, including the Trial Balance, the Balance Sheet and the Profit and Loss Account. Double-click on Financials to show this screen.

From the toolbar at the top of the Financials screen:

Select the Trial Balance icon.

You are now asked to select how you want to view the report.

For now, you will just preview the report (i.e. view it on screen). Select this and then press the [Run] button.

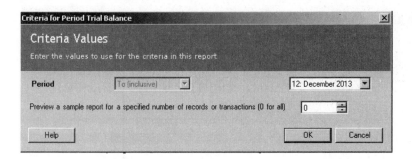

You want to view the trial balance as at December 2013, to see all of the opening balances you have entered. Make sure you amend the date box to show December 2013. Leave the next box as 0, and click [OK]

This should bring up a trial balance showing balances as at 31st December 2013. You may need to maximize the screen to see the whole report on screen – do this by clicking the *maximize* icon in the top right corner of the window ([□])

If you have entered everything correctly you should see that both columns (debit and credit) balance to **£48,018.22**.

You should now print out this trial balance and keep it safe.

Hopefully you have entered all the balances correctly and your Trial Balance is therefore correct. In the Trial Balance overleaf, however, it is apparent that there has been a mistake made in the data entry. SAGE has balanced the debits and credits by introducing a **SUSPENSE ACCOUNT** (Code 9998). On further inspection it can be seen that the figure for General Expenses (Code 8207) has been entered as £2855.64 instead of £1855.64. This must now be corrected.

There are a number of ways to make corrections in SAGE – one of the most common is via a **JOURNAL**. The journal can be entered in **COMPANY – NOMINAL LEDGER.**

Use the ⊞ Journal Entry button to enter the details of the journal.

Here a correcting journal has been produced, crediting General Expenses (Code 8207) with £1000 and debiting Suspense Account (9998) with the same amount.

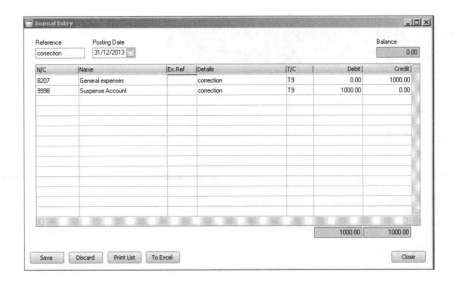

Reference	Posting Date		Details		Balance
correction	31/12/2013				0.00

N/C	Name	Ex.Ref	Details	T/C	Debit	Credit
8207	General expenses		correction	T9	0.00	1000.00
9998	Suspense Account		correction	T9	1000.00	0.00
					1000.00	1000.00

Save Discard Print List To Excel   Close

Date: 29/11/2013
Time: 13:51:20

Wynn Bowlden Tennis Coach
Period Trial Balance

Page: 1

To Period: Month 12, December 2013

N/C	Name	Debit	Credit
0030	Office Equipment	3,420.00	
0031	Office Equipment Depreciation		1,710.00
0050	Motor Vehicles	8,000.00	
0051	Motor Vehicles Depreciation		2,000.00
1001	Stock	2,865.90	
1100	Debtors Control Account	3,259.70	
1200	Bank Current Account	12,416.60	
1230	Petty Cash	100.00	
2100	Creditors Control Account		4,212.08
2202	VAT Liability		981.61
3000	Capital		3,500.00
3200	Profit and Loss Account		4,121.14
4000	Sales - Equipment		2,016.53
4001	Sales - Clothing and Footwear		2,195.46
4002	Sales - Individual coaching		13,229.30
4003	Sales - Group Coaching		13,450.50
4004	Sales - Other		601.60
5000	Purchases - Equipment	1,015.20	
5001	Purchases - Clothing and Footwear	1,310.60	
5002	Purchases - Stationery	415.20	
5003	Purchases - Packaging	208.78	
5004	Purchases - Other consumables	104.61	
7100	Rent	3,600.00	
7103	General Rates	350.00	
7304	Miscellaneous Motor Expenses	8,604.47	
7550	Telephone	491.52	
8207	General expenses	2,855.64	
9998	Suspense Account		1,000.00
	Totals:	49,018.22	49,018.22

> Notice the suspense account indicating an error

Date: 29/11/2013   **Wynn Bowlden Tennis Coach**   **Page:** 1
Time: 13:58:12   **Period Trial Balance**

To Period: Month 12, December 2013

N/C	Name	Debit	Credit
0030	Office Equipment	3,420.00	
0031	Office Equipment Depreciation		1,710.00
0050	Motor Vehicles	8,000.00	
0051	Motor Vehicles Depreciation		2,000.00
1001	Stock	2,865.90	
1100	Debtors Control Account	3,259.70	
1200	Bank Current Account	12,416.60	
1230	Petty Cash	100.00	
2100	Creditors Control Account		4,212.08
2202	VAT Liability		981.61
3000	Capital		3,500.00
3200	Profit and Loss Account		4,121.14
4000	Sales - Equipment		2,016.53
4001	Sales - Clothing and Footwear		2,195.46
4002	Sales - Individual coaching		13,229.30
4003	Sales - Group Coaching		13,450.50
4004	Sales - Other		601.60
5000	Purchases - Equipment	1,015.20	
5001	Purchases - Clothing and Footwear	1,310.60	
5002	Purchases - Stationery	415.20	
5003	Purchases - Packaging	208.78	
5004	Purchases - Other consumables	104.61	
7100	Rent	3,600.00	
7103	General Rates	350.00	
7304	Miscellaneous Motor Expenses	8,604.47	
7550	Telephone	491.52	
8207	General expenses	1,855.64	
	Totals:	48,018.22	48,018.22

> The journal has corrected the error and there is no suspense account

Entering transactions - Sales and Receipts

CONTENTS

1 Introduction

Any business will carry out a wide range of transactions every day of the week. However, the majority of these will fall into one of the following categories:

Credit transactions

- Purchases of stock on credit
- Sales of goods or services on credit

Cash transactions

- Purchases made by cash/cheque/card
- Sales made for cash/cheque/card
- Payments made to suppliers (for goods/services bought on credit)
- Receipts from customers (for goods/services sold on credit)
- Payments made to meet other expenses
- Payment of salaries and wages to staff
- Petty cash transactions
- Transactions directly through the bank account (e.g. bank charges, interest, direct debits, standing orders)

Each of these transactions will have an effect on two accounts within the SAGE system – this is the underlying principle of double-entry bookkeeping. However, SAGE simplifies this by carrying out much of the double entry automatically.

Firstly, consider the first type of transactions – purchases and sales made on credit. This means that a legally binding contract is established between the two parties, and (usually) the goods or services are supplied but payment is not made until some later date. The key document in this process is the invoice – as this is the document which demands payment and lays down the agreed terms of the transaction.

Hence entering a credit transaction (whether a purchase or a sale) is a two stage process in SAGE:

1   Enter the details of the invoice against the relevant supplier or customer. This will establish the presence and value of the legally binding debt.

2   At a later date, enter the details of the payment of the debt.

Note that this approach is applicable for both credit sales and credit purchases – you just have to be sure to enter the details in the correct part of SAGE.

Now consider the second type of transactions – each of these has a direct impact on one or other of the bank accounts within SAGE. Note that SAGE classes accounts such as cash in hand and petty cash as 'bank accounts' – they are all current assets within the Balance Sheet.

This chapter will focus on sales transactions: purchases and other transactions within the Level II syllabus will be covered in later chapters.

2   Credit sales – batching customer invoices

Wynn Bowlden has a number of credit customers on 31st December 2013. Each of these has been issued with an invoice, but these invoices now need to be entered into SAGE.

The easiest way to do this is to *batch* invoices together so that they can be input at the same time.

To enter a batch of customer (sales) invoices go to the **CUSTOMERS** module and then press the **BATCH INVOICE** button [Batch Invoice] on the screen

You will now need to insert data into the next screen as follows:

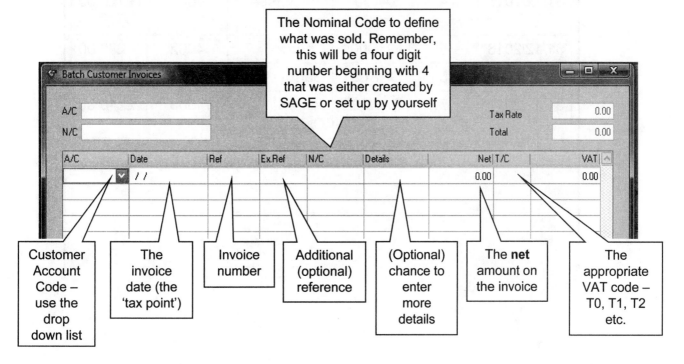

Some Important Keys / Shortcuts

F6 (found at the top of your keyboard) – *this will duplicate the field above.*

| Calc. Net | This is a really useful shortcut which can be used where you know the **gross amount** of an invoice (i.e. including VAT) but do not have the **net amount**. Simply enter the gross amount in the net box and then press the | Calc. Net | button – this will calculate the net amount and the VAT for you.

Once you have entered all invoices in the batch you should then review them to ensure you have entered them correctly, and then | Save | them.

This will post the invoices to SAGE and update the system accordingly.

Exercise

Enter the following six invoices for Wynn Bowlden using the batch invoicing method. Note that you will also have to create a new customer account for G Bates – you learned how to do this in Chapter 6.

Date	Invoice No	A/c No	Customer	Nominal Code	Net Amount
31/12/2013	1	CHA001	Chang	4001	£58.33
31/12/2013	2	CHO001	Chord	4002	£60.00
31/12/2013	3	LIT001	Little Smashers	4003	£220.00
31/12/2013	4	BAT001	Bates *(see below)*	4002	£120.00
31/12/2013	5	CHO001	Chord	4002	£30.00
31/12/2013	6	GAR001	Garros	4002	£60.00
31/12/2013	7	RAN002	Rank Outsiders	4003	£240.00

All amounts in the table are **exclusive** of VAT at 20.0%

New Customer Details

Mr G Bates
12 Main Street
Miltonby
Mellinghamshire
MN87 4DF

A/c Ref BAT001

Credit terms: Payment in 14 days

Credit Limit: £1000.00

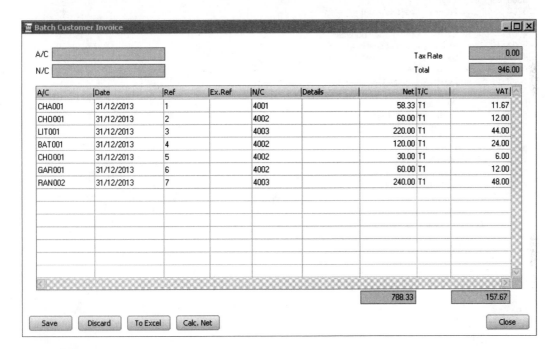

A/C	Date	Ref	Ex.Ref	N/C	Details	Net	T/C	VAT
CHA001	31/12/2013	1		4001		58.33	T1	11.67
CHO001	31/12/2013	2		4002		60.00	T1	12.00
LIT001	31/12/2013	3		4003		220.00	T1	44.00
BAT001	31/12/2013	4		4002		120.00	T1	24.00
CHO001	31/12/2013	5		4002		30.00	T1	6.00
GAR001	31/12/2013	6		4002		60.00	T1	12.00
RAN002	31/12/2013	7		4003		240.00	T1	48.00

Tax Rate 0.00
Total 946.00

788.33   157.67

Save   Discard   To Excel   Calc. Net   Close

When you have entered all seven invoices, your screen should look like this. Check for accuracy, and when you are happy press the

Save button.

Now print out another Trial Balance for December 2013. Compare the two reports and identify the changes that have occurred.

Here is a copy of the Trial Balance produced earlier:

Date: 29/11/2013   **Wynn Bowlden Tennis Coach**   **Page:** 1
Time: 13:58:12   **Period Trial Balance**

To Period: Month 12, December 2013

N/C	Name	Debit	Credit
0030	Office Equipment	3,420.00	
0031	Office Equipment Depreciation		1,710.00
0050	Motor Vehicles	8,000.00	
0051	Motor Vehicles Depreciation		2,000.00
1001	Stock	2,865.90	
1100	Debtors Control Account	3,259.70	
1200	Bank Current Account	12,416.60	
1230	Petty Cash	100.00	
2100	Creditors Control Account		4,212.08
2202	VAT Liability		981.61
3000	Capital		3,500.00
3200	Profit and Loss Account		4,121.14
4000	Sales - Equipment		2,016.53
4001	Sales - Clothing and Footwear		2,195.46
4002	Sales - Individual coaching		13,229.30
4003	Sales - Group Coaching		13,450.50
4004	Sales - Other		601.60
5000	Purchases - Equipment	1,015.20	
5001	Purchases - Clothing and Footwear	1,310.60	
5002	Purchases - Stationery	415.20	
5003	Purchases - Packaging	208.78	
5004	Purchases - Other consumables	104.61	
7100	Rent	3,600.00	
7103	General Rates	350.00	
7304	Miscellaneous Motor Expenses	8,604.47	
7550	Telephone	491.52	
8207	General expenses	1,855.64	
	Totals:	48,018.22	48,018.22

This is a copy of the new trial balance:

Date:	11/12/2013	**Wynn Bowlden Tennis Coach**		Page: 1
Time:	16:38:43	**Period Trial Balance**		

To Period: Month 12, December 2013

N/C	Name		Debit	Credit	
0030	Office Equipment		3,420.00		
0031	Office Equipment Depreciation			1,710.00	
0050	Motor Vehicles		8,000.00		
0051	Motor Vehicles Depreciation			2,000.00	
1001	Stock		2,865.90		
1100	Debtors Control Account	❶	4,205.70		
1200	Bank Current Account		12,416.60		
1230	Petty Cash		100.00		
2100	Creditors Control Account			4,212.08	
2200	Sales Tax Control Account			157.67	❷
2202	VAT Liability			981.61	
3000	Capital			3,500.00	
3200	Profit and Loss Account			4,121.14	
4000	Sales - Equipment			2,016.53	
4001	Sales - Clothing and Footwear			2,253.79	❸
4002	Sales - Individual Coaching			13,499.30	
4003	Sales - Group Coaching			13,910.50	
4004	Sales - Other			601.60	
5000	Purchases - Equipment		1,015.20		
5001	Purchases - Clothing and Footwear		1,310.60		
5002	Purchases - Stationery		415.20		
5003	Purchases - Packaging		208.78		
5004	Purchases - Other Consumables		104.61		
7100	Rent		3,600.00		
7103	General Rates		350.00		
7304	Miscellaneous Motor Expenses		8,604.47		
7550	Telephone		491.52		
8207	General expenses		1,855.64		
		Totals:	48,964.22	48,964.22	

Notice which figures have changed.

(1)   N/C 1100 (Debtors control account) has increased to £4205.70. This reflects the fact that Wynn Bowlden is now owed an additional £946.00 by its debtors.

(2)   There is a new Nominal Code (2200) called 'Sales Tax Control Account'. This control account automatically records all output VAT (on sales). There is a similar control account for input VAT (on purchases). The two control accounts are used to calculate and produce the company's VAT Return. The amount on this code is currently £157.67 (a **credit** balance) – the VAT charged on all the sales invoices you have entered.

(3)   N/Cs 4001, 4002 and 4003 have increased, representing the new sales that the company made on 31st December. Note that the increase in these figures is the **net** increase in sales.

The increase in **debit** entries (£946.00) equals the increase in **credit** entries (£788.33 plus £157.67) – the principles of double entry bookkeeping have been met and SAGE has actually done the double entries for you.

3 Credit sales – trade and cash discounts

A business may decide to offer a trade discount to regular customers: a trade discount is a set % discount on the normal sales price of the goods. The VAT is calculated on the value of the sale less the discount and the sales invoice will show the value of the sale net of the trade discount.

Cash, or settlement, discounts can also be offered to encourage customers to pay promptly: a cash discount is a fixed % discount which can be deducted by the customer from the invoice value, as long as the invoice is paid within a set period of time. This discount may or may not be taken up by the customer and so is not deducted on the face of the sales invoice. However, the VAT will still be calculated on the value of the sale less the cash discount, whether the discount is taken or not.

Example

Wynn has issued an invoice to Annette Chord as per the details below. Wynn has agreed to increase her credit limit to £2,000 and to offer her a 3% cash discount if the invoice is paid within 7 days to encourage prompt payment.

Date	Invoice No	A/c No	Customer	Nominal Code	Net Amount
31/12/2013	8	CHO001	Annette Chord	4000	£600.00

When entering this invoice on SAGE, you will need to remember that the VAT is calculated on the value of the sale less the discount.

This means that the vatable amount of the invoice will be:

Sales price	£600.00
Cash discount	(£18.00)
	————
Vatable sales price	**£582.00**

Output vat: £582.00 × 20% = £116.40.

The invoice will then be entered on SAGE, using the batching method, as shown below:

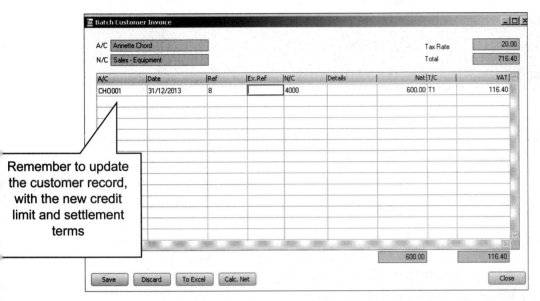

The cash discount will be accounted for as a separate exercise if it is subsequently taken by the customer – this is illustrated later in this chapter.

Example

Wynn Bowlden has invoiced a new customer, Gary String, as below. She has decided to offer him a 3% trade discount on all sales, and a 2% cash discount if the invoice is paid within 7 days.

New customer details

Gary String   **A/c Ref : STR001**
Mr Gary String
11 High Road
Miltonby
Mellinghamshire
MN15 1FT

Credit Terms: **Payment in 28 days**   **Credit Limit £5000**

Trade discount: **3%**

Cash discount: **2% 7 days**

Date	Invoice No	A/c No	Customer	Nominal Code	Net Amount
31/12/2013	9	STR001	Gary String	4000	£2000

The vatable amount of the invoice is as follows:

Sales price	£2000.00
Trade discount	(£60.00)
Net sales price	£1,940.00
Settlement discount	(£38.80)
Vatable sales price	**£1,901.20**

Vat on sales price: £1901.20 × 20% = £380.24.

The net sales value to enter on SAGE will be £1,940.00 – remember, we never show trade discounts in the accounts.

This should be entered on SAGE as shown below.

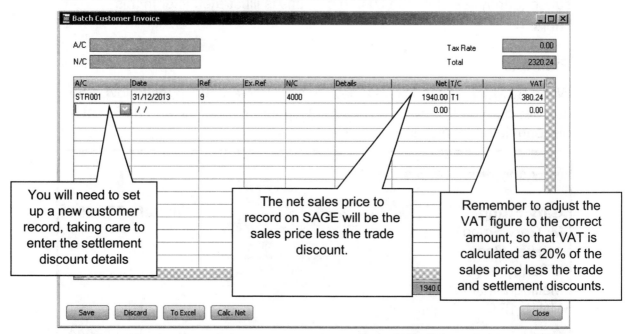

The settlement discount will then be entered on SAGE when the invoice is paid by the customer. This is covered later in this chapter.

4 Producing sales invoices and credit notes

As well as entering sales invoices on SAGE using the batch invoice method described above, SAGE also offers the facility to generate sales invoices using the Sales Invoice wizard in the Customers module.

This wizard can be used to generate sales invoices, automatically numbered by SAGE, which can then be printed off to send to customers. SAGE will calculate any discounts due based on details entered in the relevant customer account, and will also calculate the VAT on the invoice, taking into account any discounts applicable. The invoice will then be automatically posted to the debtors control account and to the sales account.

By comparison, the batching method is used to enter details manually from sales invoices which have already been generated by a means other than SAGE.

To generate a new invoice, you will need to select the icon in the Customers module and then work through the various screens.

The first screen allows you to enter key details to appear on the invoice.

When you select the customer account number, SAGE will complete the customer address, credit terms and settlement discount details as set up in the Customer Record on SAGE.

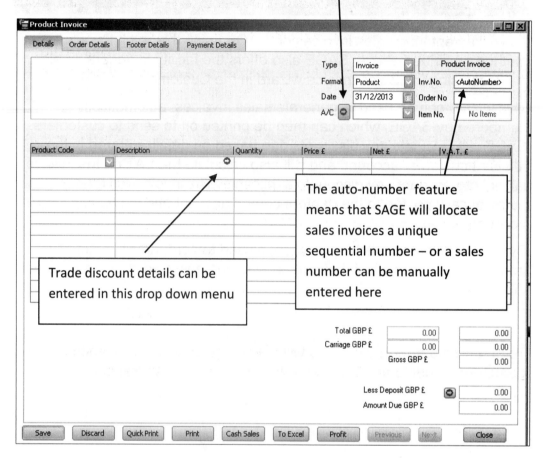

Trade discount details can be entered in this drop down menu

The auto-number feature means that SAGE will allocate sales invoices a unique sequential number – or a sales number can be manually entered here

Various other details can be entered on the sales invoice as required by working through the remaining screens.

The sales invoice can be printed by using the Print button: SAGE will then ask you to set a default layout for your invoice.

Remember to save the invoice. You will then need to select [Update Ledgers] on the Customer Process screen so that it is posted by SAGE to the ledgers.

The New Credit option in the Customers module also allows sales credit notes to be generated in the same way as the New Invoice option above. Again, SAGE will generate a sales credit that can be printed and sent to customers, and will also automatically make the correct entries to post the transaction in the accounts.

5 Posting credit notes

A credit note is essentially a 'negative invoice' and is produced and sent to customers when a refund of money is needed. The most likely time this will happen is when goods that the organization has sold to a customer have been returned as faulty. Credit notes can also be used to correct errors.

Producing a credit note in SAGE is straightforward and effectively mirrors the process for producing an invoice.

Let us suppose that the coaching session booked by Annette Chord (Invoice Number 5), for which she paid £30.00 plus VAT, is cancelled and Wynn Bowlden agrees to issue a credit note to the customer.

From the **CUSTOMER** module select **CUSTOMER LIST.**

From the icons at the top of the screen select the **Batch Credit** icon.

Here you can enter a batch of Credit Notes (just as you did with the batched invoices). SAGE shows your entries in RED to make it obvious that this is a Credit Note.

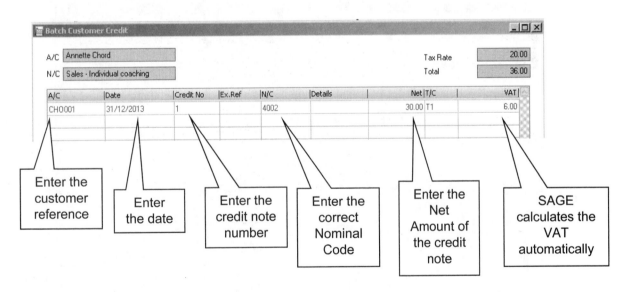

When you have entered all Credit Notes in the batch, and checked their accuracy, **SAVE** them to ensure that SAGE can process them.

6 Producing customer statements

Having produced and sent invoices to customers, most businesses will also need to send periodic (usually monthly) statements to their customers which will list all new transactions – such as new purchases, payments received, credit notes issued etc.

SAGE allows the easy creation and production of customer statements.

Firstly, from the **CUSTOMER** module, press the Statements button.

You may need to change the view in the CUSTOMER module first –make sure that the "Customer option" is ticked:

You will then need to choose the layout option in the pop up box: SAGE will then remember this as your "favourite" if you click on the star next to the document name.

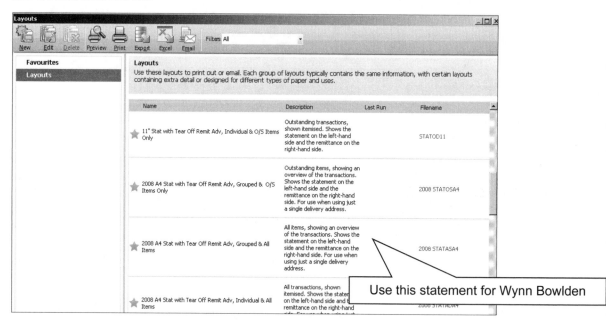

Use this statement for Wynn Bowlden

This provides a choice of different statement layouts. You should use the one which best suits your business needs; however, for the purposes of this manual you should use the one called 'A4 Stat with Tear off Remit. Adv. Grouped & All Items'. Select this one by double-clicking.

In the **CRITERIA VALUES** screen (see below) use the pull-down menus to select customer Chord (Ref CHO001). You can use the 'From...to...' feature to select a range of customers – but for now just select the one.

Make sure the Transaction dates are '01/12/2013' to '31/12/2013' – this will ensure that all transactions in December are shown.

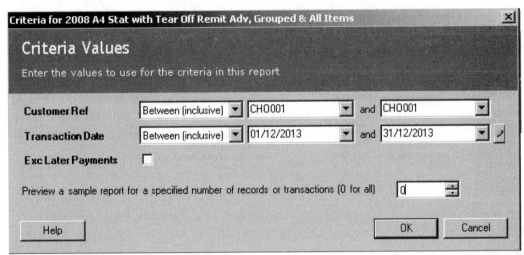

Press [OK] to create the report.

This statement (shown on the next page) could then be printed out (using special stationery if required) and then sent to the customer.

Wynn Bowlden Tennis Coach
15 Love Street
Pickerton
Mellinghamshire
ML40 3TT

Wynn Bowlden Tennis Coach
15 Love Street
Pickerton
Mellinghamshire
ML40 3TT

Annette Chord   CHO001
20 New York Street
Bridgeford   31/12/2013
Mellinghamshire
BG16 9JY
                       1

Annette Chord   CHO001
20 New York Street
Bridgeford   31/12/2013
Mellinghamshire
BG16 9JY
                       1

NOTE: All values are shown in Pound Sterling   **NOTE: All values are shown in Pound Sterling**

31/12/13 O/Bal	Goods/Services	819.20 *	
31/12/13 2	Goods/Services	72.00 *	
31/12/13 5	Goods/Services	36.00 *	
31/12/13 8	Goods/Services	716.40 *	
31/12/13 1	Credit	*	36.00

31/12/13	Goods/Services	819.20	
31/12/13	Goods/Services	72.00	
31/12/13	Goods/Services	36.00	
31/12/13	Goods/Services	716.40	
31/12/13	Credit		36.00

£   1,607.60 £   0.00 £   0.00 £   0.00 £   0.00

£   1,607.60   £   1,607.60

7 Recording receipts

The most likely sources of receipts for most businesses are:

- Cash sales (including sales of fixed assets)
- Receipts from debtors

You will look at these in turn.

Cash sales

Wynn Bowlden also sells items to two customers who pay cash on 31st December 2013. The first of these is a pair of trainers for £30.00 plus VAT; the second is for a dozen tennis balls for £9.00 plus VAT.

Wynn Bowlden has decided to use the 'bank' account called 'Cash Register'. This will be used to record the payments into and out of the cash register. Use Nominal Code 1235 for this.

From the **BANK** window, use the 'blue bar' to highlight code 1235 then click the ▨ icon.
Bank
Receipts

Enter the two cash sales as below:

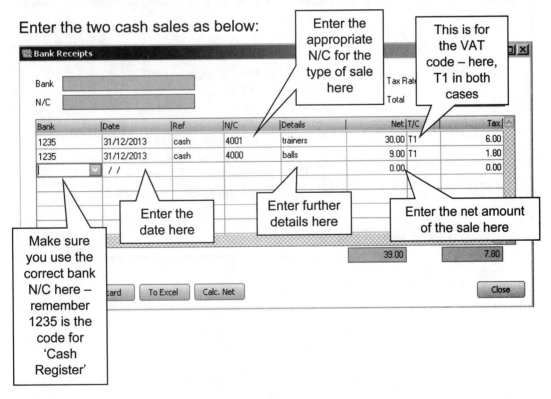

When you have entered both transactions press **SAVE**.

You should now see that there is a balance on N/C 1235 of £46.80 – the total amount of the two cash sales.

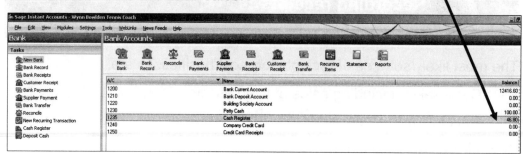

Sales of Fixed Assets

When a fixed asset is sold, the sales proceeds received need to be accounted for in the nominal code 4200: Sales of Assets. This ensures that the sale is shown separately from those sales made in the normal course of business.

Wynn Bowlden sells a computer for £120 cash (including VAT) to Ann Smith on 31st December 2013.

This can be entered using the Bank Receipts icon as before:

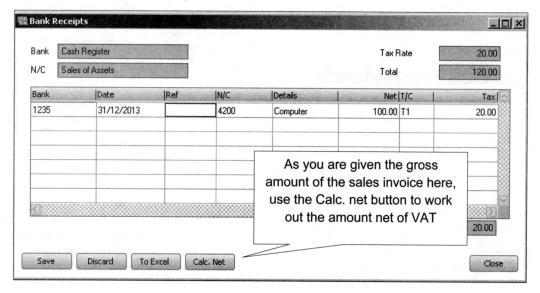

8 Receipts from customers

On 31st December Wynn Bowlden also received two amounts from customers in respect of their outstanding invoices. These were:

Rank Outsiders   Cheque for £1820.49

Noah Chang   Cash £50.00

To enter these, firstly click the icon from within the **BANK** module, or from within the **CUSTOMER** module.

Then enter the details of the first receipt as follows.

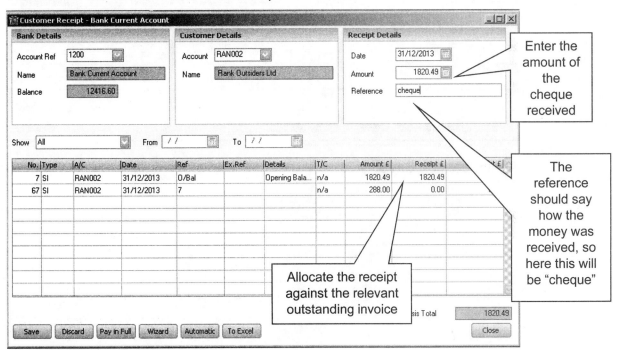

Click **Save** to post this entry to SAGE.

Now enter the second receipt, from Noah Chang. Note that only £50.00 has been received, and that he paid in cash.

Your screen should look like this (note that the bank account has changed from 1200 to 1235):

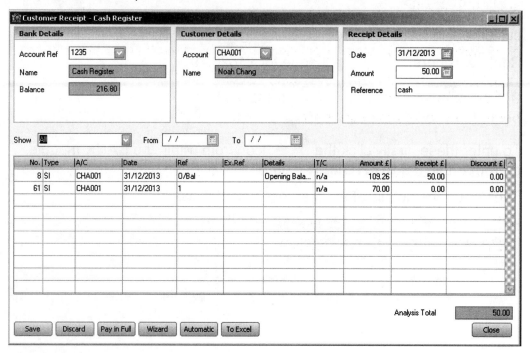

Again, click on **Save.**

Entering discounts

When a customer deducts a trade discount, this will be not be entered as a separate item on SAGE: instead you will deduct any trade discount from the net sales value of the invoice when you enter it on SAGE, as you did in section 3 above.

However, any settlement (cash) discount taken by a customer will need to be entered on SAGE as a separate item at the same time as the receipt.

Wynn Bowlden receives a cheque for £2281.44 from Gary String on 31st December. This includes the settlement discount of £38.80 which has been deducted by the customer.

To enter this on SAGE, firstly click the Customer Receipt icon from within the **BANK** module.

Then enter the details of the receipt and the discount as follows.

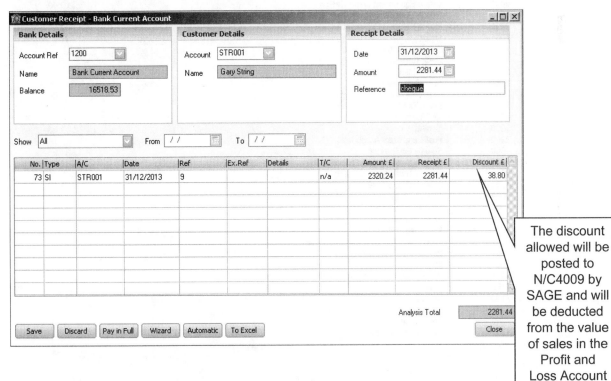

The discount allowed will be posted to N/C4009 by SAGE and will be deducted from the value of sales in the Profit and Loss Account

Your customer list should now look like this:

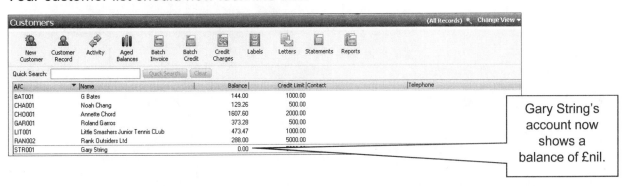

Gary String's account now shows a balance of £nil.

BACS Receipts

When recording BACS receipts the same process should be followed. However, the date that the amount is received in the bank should be recorded as the date on SAGE, and the reference on SAGE should generally be the name of the supplier so it ties in with what appears on the bank statement. This makes it easier to perform the bank reconciliation (covered at Level III of your studies).

You should now produce a revised Trial Balance. Make sure yours matches with the one below:

Date: 25/06/2014	**Wynn Bowlden Tennis Coach**		Page: 1
Time: 15:19:33	**Period Trial Balance**		

To Period: Month 12, December 2013

N/C	Name	Debit	Credit
0030	Office Equipment	3,420.00	
0031	Office Equipment Depreciation		1,710.00
0050	Motor Vehicles	8,000.00	
0051	Motor Vehicles Depreciation		2,000.00
1001	Stock	2,865.90	
1100	Debtors Control Account	3,015.61	
1200	Bank Current Account	16,518.53	
1230	Petty Cash	100.00	
1235	Cash Register	216.80	
2100	Creditors Control Account		4,212.08
2200	Sales Tax Control Account		676.11
2202	VAT Liability		981.61
3000	Capital		3,500.00
3200	Profit and Loss Account		4,121.14
4000	Sales - Equipment		4,565.53
4001	Sales - Clothing and Footwear		2,283.79
4002	Sales - Individual Coaching		13,469.30
4003	Sales - Group Coaching		13,910.50
4004	Sales - Other		601.60
4009	Discounts Allowed	38.80	
4200	Sales of Assets		100.00
5000	Purchases - Equipment	1,015.20	
5001	Purchases- Clothing and Footwear	1,310.60	
5002	Purchases - Stationery	415.20	
5003	Purchases - Packaging	208.78	
5004	Purchases - Other consumables	104.61	
7100	Rent	3,600.00	
7103	General Rates	350.00	
7304	Miscellaneous Motor Expenses	8,604.47	
7550	Telephone	491.52	
8207	General expenses	1,855.64	
	Totals:	52,131.66	52,131.6

> Make sure your discount allowed figure agrees to this one

Entering transactions – purchases and payments

1 Introduction

In this chapter we will look at how to enter supplier invoices and credit notes, and how to process bank and cash payments.

2 Credit purchases

When an organisation purchases goods or services on credit, it will receive an invoice from the supplier. Invoices must be recorded immediately in SAGE, even though they may not be paid for some time.

The most common way to process supplier invoices is to *batch* them (in much the same way as you did with the invoices to customers). This way, a number of invoices can be processed at the same time.

The process for entering batches of supplier invoices is very similar to that for entering batches of customer invoices – except it is accessed via the **SUPPLIERS** module.

You should enter the **SUPPLIERS** module now.

Press the icon in the Supplier module.

Wynn Bowlden received the following five invoices on 31st December 2013.

Invoice Ref	Invoice Date	Supplier	Account	Net amount	Nominal Code
1892	29/12/13	Kike Shoes	KS001	£308.30	5001
309	29/12/13	First Serve Office Supplies	FS001	£220.00	5002
312	29/12/13	First Serve Office Supplies	FS001	£16.58	5002
2018	30/12/13	Wotta Rackets Ltd	WR001	£190.00	5000
40293	30/12/13	Wilkinson Tennis Balls	WT001	£49.50	5000

You should now enter the above five supplier invoices as a batch. You should use the **Invoice Date** shown above, rather than the date the invoice is actually received.

When you have done this the screen should look like this:

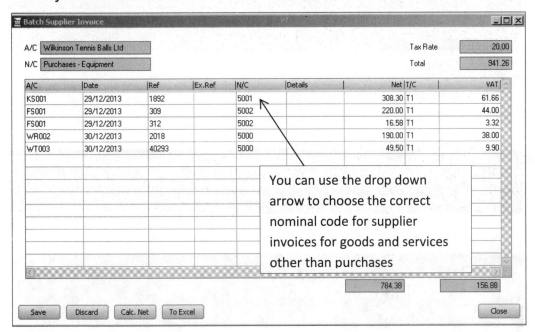

You should verify the entries and then press the **SAVE** button to post your entries to SAGE.

3 Supplier credit notes

These are processed in exactly the same way as you processed credit notes issued to customers.

Access the entry screen from the SUPPLIERS module, using the Batch Credit button.

Wynn Bowlden receives one credit note. It is from First Serve Office Supplies on 31 December and is a credit for £49.99 (excluding VAT) for some items that were returned as faulty. The credit note reference is 129C. The Nominal Code for this is 5002 (Purchases – Stationery).

You should enter this as follows:

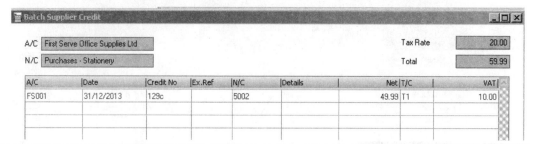

Again – note that SAGE shows your entries in red so that they are easily identifiable as a credit note. When you have checked the accuracy of your entries you should press the **SAVE** button.

4 Bank transactions

SAGE allows you to run a number of 'bank accounts'. These need not necessarily all be held at a bank – they could also include cash in hand, petty cash etc.

The principles for making payments into or out of any of these accounts are the same.

Enter the **Bank** module. You can see that SAGE has already set up a number of different bank accounts, each with its own Nominal Code. You can of course amend these or add to them if you wish.

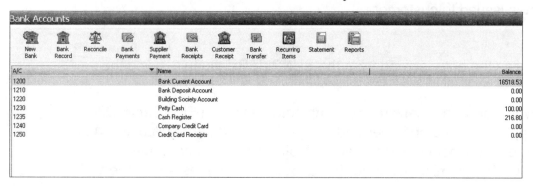

The most commonly used bank account is probably Nominal Code 1200. This is the one that you will use in this manual for payments into and out of Wynn Bowlden's main current bank account. You can see that it has a balance at the moment of £16518.53.

5 Making payments

Wynn Bowlden has three payments to make on 31st December 2013. These are:

- A cheque for £102.35 (plus VAT at 20%) to Arrow Telecoms to pay the telephone bill – Cheque number 249

- A cheque for £35.00 to Pickerton Darts Association for advertising in their League Handbook (no VAT on this transaction) – Cheque number 250

- A cheque for £50.00 to Pickerton Borough Council for a parking permit (no VAT) – Cheque number 251

To enter these transactions, go to the **BANK** module, select the required bank account (in this case the current account) and click the   button, or select **BANK PAYMENTs** from the Tasks Panel.

Enter each transaction as a separate line. Be careful to make sure you select the appropriate Nominal Code for the expense item, and also the correct VAT rate. If there is no VAT you should use Tax Code **T0**.

Your entries should look like this:

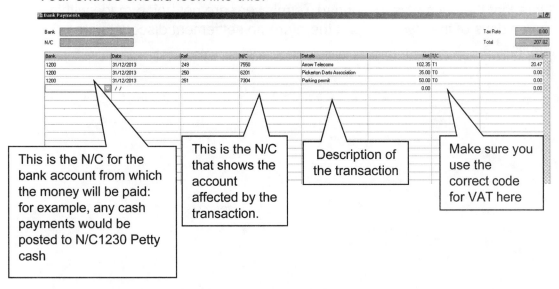

When you have checked your entries, **SAVE** them to SAGE.

Note that any cash payments would also be entered by following the same method and using the nominal code N/C1230 for the bank account from which the money will be paid.

Now check the balance on Nominal Code 1200 (the bank current account).

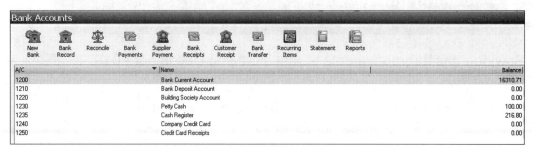

See how the bank balance has now gone down to £16310.71 – reflecting the fact that payments of £207.82 (£187.35 plus £20.47 VAT) have been taken from it.

Paying suppliers

Wynn Bowlden also decides to pay two outstanding creditors on 31st December, as follows:

First Serve Office Supplies (FS001)
Amount: £401.35 inc VAT   *Paid by cheque number 252*

Yonnad Tenniswear (YT001)
Amount £864.10 (inc VAT).   *Paid by cheque number 253*

Note that the payments to Yonnad Tenniswear are not being made within seven days of the invoices, and therefore no settlement discounts are applicable.

To enter these payments onto SAGE click the 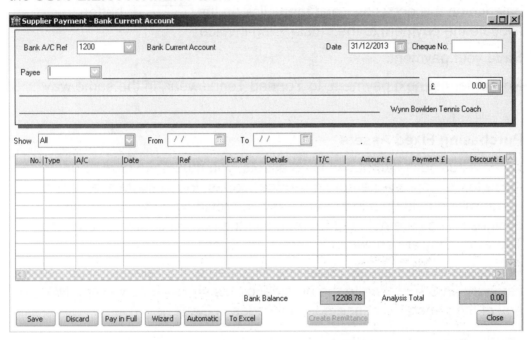 Supplier Payment button from the **BANK** window, or, alternatively, go to the **SUPPLIER** window and click on the **SUPPLIER PAYMENT** task.

Use the drop down menu to select the first supplier to pay – in this case First Serve Office Supplies. Enter the correct date, the cheque number and the amount being paid (£401.35).

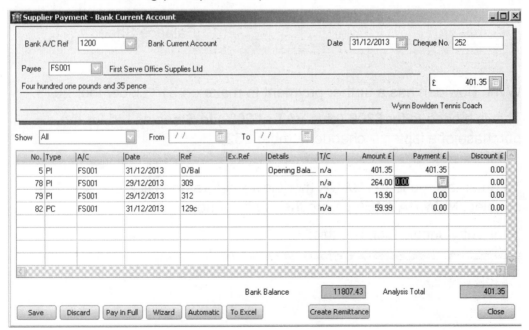

Note how SAGE has completed the bottom half of the screen with the outstanding invoices for this supplier. This allows you to decide which outstanding invoices you want to pay.

Click on the line showing the invoice to be paid – this is the opening balance on this occasion - and then click on the ⌈Pay in Full⌋ button to allocate the payment to the outstanding invoice.

Save your payment.

Now enter the next payment, to Yonnad Tenniswear, in the same way.

Purchasing Fixed Assets

When a business purchases fixed assets, you must take care to enter these to the appropriate nominal ledger codes. Fixed asset are assets which will be held on a long term basis in providing a service to the business. They are not held for resale in the normal course of trading. Therefore they are shown in the Balance Sheet.

Purchases of fixed assets should be allocated to the relevant fixed asset category on SAGE – so to the nominal codes shown below - (and NOT to any of the general expense nominal codes in SAGE).

Fixed Assets	Low
Property	0010
Plant and Machinery	0020
Office Equipment	0030
Furniture and Fixtures	0040
Motor Vehicles	0050

Using these nominal codes will ensure that the fixed asset purchased will be correctly shown in the Balance Sheet

Wynn Bowlden has a further payment to make on 31st December 2013.

This is a cheque for £300 (plus VAT at 20%) to Steeples Ltd for the purchase of a laptop – cheque number 252

To enter this, go to the **BANK** module as before and click the Bank Payments button, or select **NEW PAYMENT** from the Tasks panel.

Your entry should look like this:

Bank	Date	Ref	N/C	Details	Net	T/C	Tax
1200	31/12/2013	252	0030	Steeples Ltd - Laptop	300.00	T1	60.00
	/ /				0.00		0.00

6   Checking bank activity

It is important for businesses to regularly check their bank transactions. There are a number of reasons for this:

- To monitor the bank balance to ensure that there is sufficient money to meet liabilities

- To monitor transactions to ensure against fraud or theft

- To ensure there is not too much money in any particular account. For example, if the balance in the current account reaches a certain level the business may decide to transfer some of it to a different account where it may earn a higher rate of interest.

Checking the activity on a bank account is straightforward.

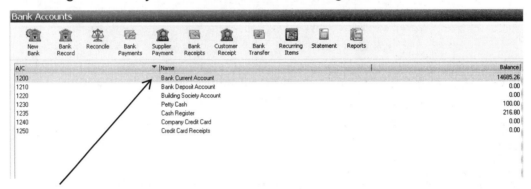

Highlight the account you want to check, and then double-click on it with the mouse.

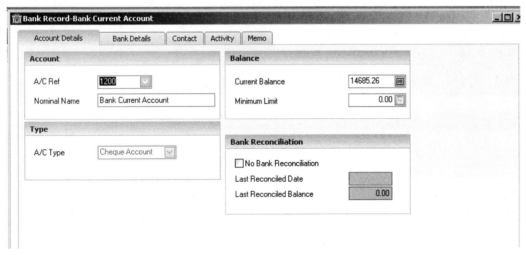

Choose the [Activity] tab at the top.

You should now see the following screen.

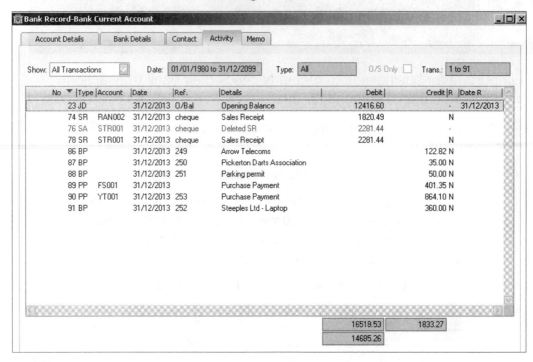

This shows all the transactions to date affecting N/C 1200 (the main current account). Make sure you can identify all of these.

Further details of individual transactions can be obtained by clicking on the Show Details button.

Note that Debit entries represent monies paid **into** the bank account; credit entries show payments **out of** the bank account.

Exercise

Now produce an activity report for account 1235 ('Cash Register'). It should look like this:

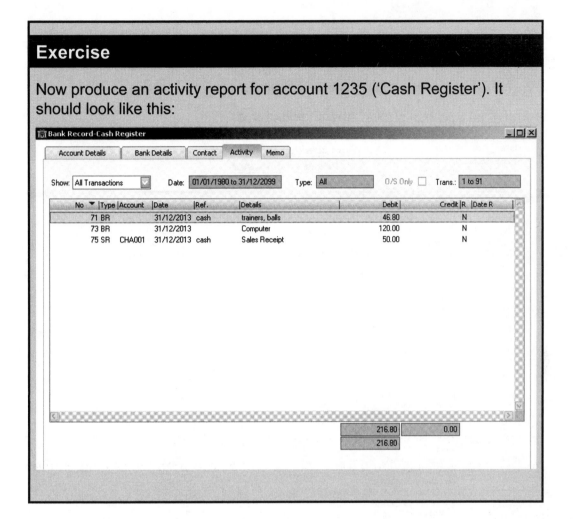

Exercise

You should now produce a revised Trial Balance.

Your Trial Balance should now look like this.

Date: 25/06/2014   **Wynn Bowlden Tennis Coach**   **Page:** 1
Time: 16:38:11   **Period Trial Balance**

To Period: Month 12, December 2013

N/C	Name	Debit	Credit
0030	Office Equipment	3,720.00	
0031	Office Equipment Depreciation		1,710.00
0050	Motor Vehicles	8,000.00	
0051	Motor Vehicles Depreciation		2,000.00
1001	Stock	2,865.90	
1100	Debtors Control Account	3,015.61	
1200	Bank Current Account	14,685.26	
1230	Petty Cash	100.00	
1235	Cash Register	216.80	
2100	Creditors Control Account		3,827.90
2200	Sales Tax Control Account		676.11
2201	Purchase Tax Control Account	227.35	
2202	VAT Liability		981.61
3000	Capital		3,500.00
3200	Profit and Loss Account		4,121.14
4000	Sales - Equipment		4,565.53
4001	Sales - Clothing and Footwear		2,283.79
4002	Sales - Individual Coaching		13,469.30
4003	Sales - Group Coaching		13,910.50
4004	Sales - Other		601.60
4009	Discounts Allowed	38.80	
4200	Sales of Assets		100.00
5000	Purchases - Equipment	1,254.70	
5001	Purchases- Clothing and Footwear	1,618.90	
5002	Purchases - Stationery	601.79	
5003	Purchases - Packaging	208.78	
5004	Purchases - Other consumables	104.61	
6201	Advertising	35.00	
7100	Rent	3,600.00	
7103	General Rates	350.00	
7304	Miscellaneous Motor Expenses	8,654.47	
7550	Telephone	593.87	
8207	General expenses	1,855.64	
	Totals:	51,747.48	51,747.48

7 Transfers

Sometimes a business may transfer money from one account to another. For example, it may transfer money from 'Cash Register' to the 'Current Bank Account'. Alternatively, it may transfer an amount from the current account to a deposit account. It may also need to reimburse the petty cash account with money from the current account or cash in hand.

From the **Bank** module click the [Bank Transfer icon] icon.

Wynn Bowlden operates a petty cash tin, to be used for items such as stamps, milk, tea, coffee, taxi fares etc.

An *IMPREST* system is operated, with an imprest amount of £100. However, she decides that this is too low an amount and so decides to increase the imprest amount to £200. She therefore takes £100 from the bank current account and puts it in the petty cash tin.

You should enter the details of this transfer as below and then **Save.**

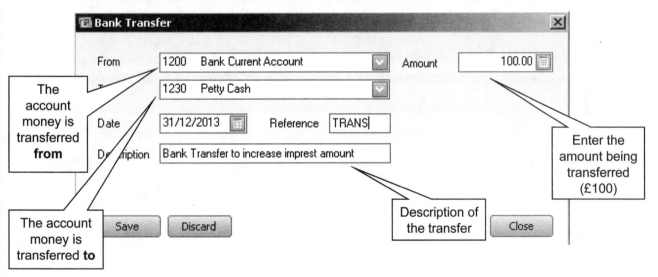

8   Recurring transactions

A business will often also have recurring transactions, such as standing orders or direct debits. These represent regular payments into or out of a bank account. SAGE allows you to set these up so that you do not have to enter them each month.

On 1st December, Wynn Bowlden signs a contract to advertise on North East Radio for the next twelve months. The cost for this is £120 plus VAT per month. This will be collected by direct debit from the main current bank account, with the first payment being taken on 31st December, and on the last day of each month after that.

To enter this into SAGE as a recurring transaction, click the icon from the **Bank** module. Click Add to enter a new recurring entry. Now enter the details of the transaction as per the previous page.

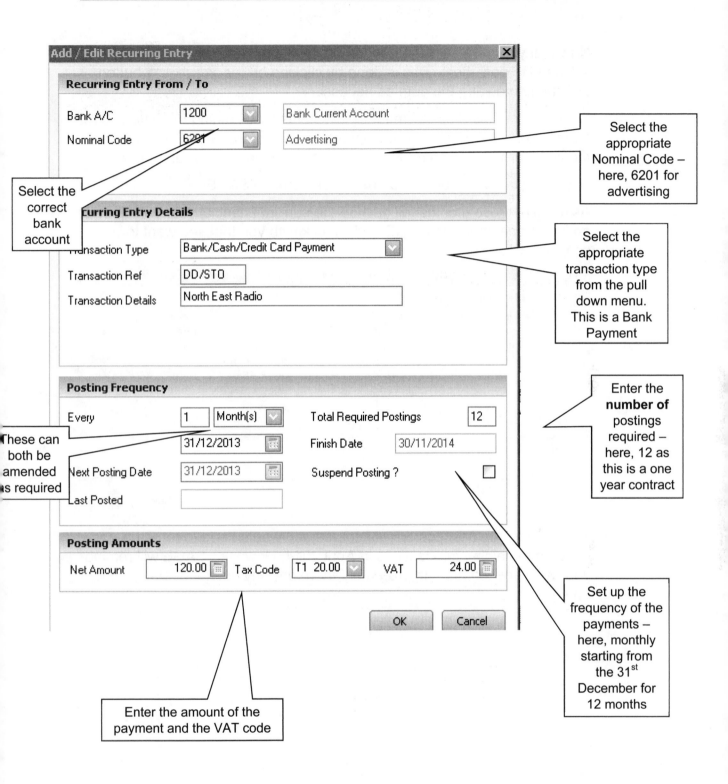

Now that you have set up the recurring entry for these payments, you will still need to post them. This is done by clicking on the Process button and then amending the date as necessary.

For now, post the first four month's payments by changing the date to 31st March 2014. Press the TAB key on the keyboard and SAGE will bring up the first four months' payments (December, January, February, March).

Click the Post button to post these items to SAGE.

As three of these months fall outside the current financial year (which ends on 31st December 2013) SAGE will check with you that you want to continue. Click yes.

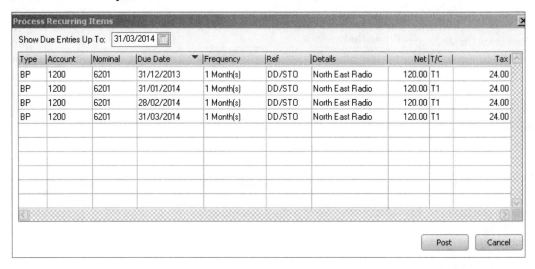

These items are now posted – of course you would need to remember to post the remaining transactions in April 2014. However, SAGE will remind you when you load up the program if there are any outstanding recurring entries to post.

Petty Cash

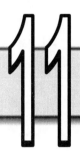

CONTENTS

1 Introduction

Most businesses use petty cash as a way of paying for minor expenses such as taxi fares, tea, milk and coffee, window cleaning etc.

We have already seen that Wynn Bowlden operates a petty cash tin with an imprest amount of £200.

In this chapter you will learn how to enter petty cash transactions.

2 Petty cash payments

Payments out of petty cash are recorded in exactly the same way as any other payments made from a bank account. Remember to make sure that you use the correct account number (1230).

Also be sure to enter the correct VAT code for each transaction. Many items commonly paid for out of petty cash are zero-rated or exempt – but not all.

Wynn Bowlden makes the following payments out of petty cash on 31st December 2013.

Voucher No	Description	Amount	VAT?
204	Tea and milk	£3.65	Zero Rated (use tax code T0)
205	Newspapers	£4.00	Zero Rated (T0)
206	Stamps	£5.60	Exempt (T2)
207	Bus Fare	£5.00	Zero rated (T0)
208	Pens	£2.99	VAT inclusive at 20%

Enter these by clicking on the Bank Payments button.

Make sure that the account selected is 1230 – petty cash.

Enter each of the transactions above.

Your screen should look like this:

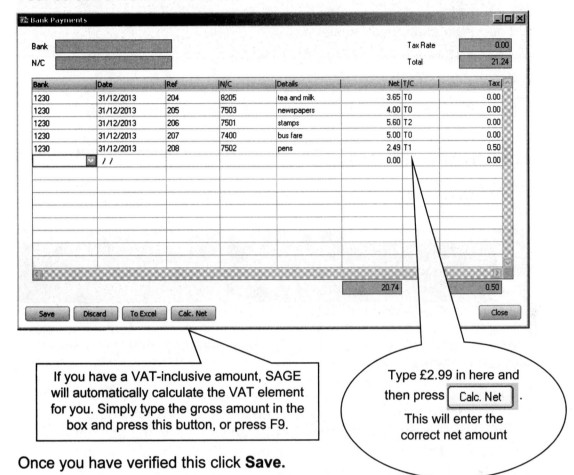

If you have a VAT-inclusive amount, SAGE will automatically calculate the VAT element for you. Simply type the gross amount in the box and press this button, or press F9.

Type £2.99 in here and then press Calc. Net . This will enter the correct net amount

Once you have verified this click **Save.**

A word about VAT

Value Added Tax (VAT) is a tax imposed on consumers. Whilst you do not need to understand fully at this stage the intricacies of VAT you should have an awareness of the different rates which can be applied.

Most goods and services are taxed at the **STANDARD** rate of VAT (currently 20%). In SAGE, these transactions are given a tax code of T1.

Some goods and services are completely **EXEMPT** from VAT – such as postage stamps. These are given a tax code of T2.

A limited number of goods and services are taxable under VAT, but are currently taxed at 0% – these are **ZERO-RATED**. These are given a tax code of T0. Examples include some food and drink, children's clothes and newspapers.

A number of transactions are **OUTSIDE THE SCOPE** of VAT – such as wages payments. These do not need to appear on the VAT return and are given a tax code of T9.

There are other variations to tax codes and SAGE allows you to easily amend the tax codes and rates applied (for example if the government announces a change in the standard VAT Rate).

Further information on how SAGE deals with VAT can be found by accessing the SAGE Help Facility and then searching for VAT.

<u>F</u>ile   <u>E</u>dit   <u>V</u>iew   M<u>o</u>dules   Sett<u>i</u>ngs   <u>T</u>ools   <u>W</u>ebLinks   <u>N</u>ews Feeds   <u>H</u>elp

For more information on VAT itself you should contact Her Majesty's Revenue and Customs (HMRC), view the website <u>www.hmrc.gov.uk</u>, or speak to an accountant.

3   Reimbursing the petty cash account

To reimburse the petty cash account, simply transfer the money from one account (usually tl ⬚ rent account or cash in hand) to the petty cash account using the ⬚ Bank Transf button.

Wynn Bowlden reimbursed the petty cash tin at the end of 31st December 2013 with the amount necessary to bring the float back to £200.00. The amount spent during the day was £21.24 and so this is the amount to be reimbursed. This money was taken from the 'Cash Register' account.

The transfer entry should look like this:

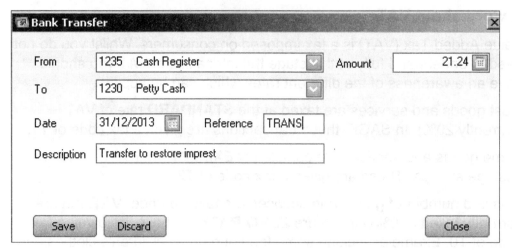

KAPLAN PUBLISHING

You should now also see that the balance on the petty cash account has been restored to £200, whilst the balance of cash in hand shown in the Cash Register account is now £195.56.

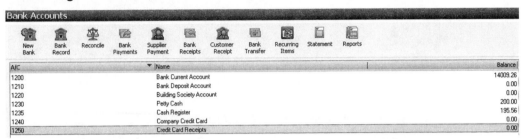

A/C	Name	Balance
1200	Bank Current Account	14009.26
1210	Bank Deposit Account	0.00
1220	Building Society Account	0.00
1230	Petty Cash	200.00
1235	Cash Register	195.56
1240	Company Credit Card	0.00
1250	Credit Card Receipts	0.00

You have now learnt how to process the vast majority of transactions that most businesses will deal with on a day to day basis.

You should now print off a Trial Balance for December 2013, which should look like the one reproduced below.

Date: 26/06/2014   **Wynn Bowlden Tennis Coach**   Page: 1
Time: 11:45:54   **Period Trial Balance**

To Period: Month 12, December 2013

N/C	Name	Debit	Credit
0030	Office Equipment	3,720.00	
0031	Office Equipment Depreciation		1,710.00
0050	Motor Vehicles	8,000.00	
0051	Motor Vehicles Depreciation		2,000.00
1001	Stock	2,865.90	
1100	Debtors Control Account	3,015.61	
1200	Bank Current Account	14,441.26	
1230	Petty Cash	200.00	
1235	Cash Register	195.56	
2100	Creditors Control Account		3,827.90
2200	Sales Tax Control Account		676.11
2201	Purchase Tax Control Account	251.85	
2202	VAT Liability		981.61
3000	Capital		3,500.00
3200	Profit and Loss Account		4,121.14
4000	Sales - Equipment		4,565.53
4001	Sales - Clothing and Footwear		2,283.79
4002	Sales - Individual Coaching		13,469.30
4003	Sales - Group Coaching		13,910.50
4004	Sales - Other		601.60
4009	Discounts Allowed	38.80	
4200	Sales of Assets		100.00
5000	Purchases - Equipment	1,254.70	
5001	Purchases- Clothing and Footwear	1,618.90	
5002	Purchases - Stationery	601.79	
5003	Purchases - Packaging	208.78	
5004	Purchases - Other consumables	104.61	
6201	Advertising	155.00	
7100	Rent	3,600.00	
7103	General Rates	350.00	
7304	Miscellaneous Motor Expenses	8,654.47	
7400	Travelling	5.00	
7501	Postage and Carriage	5.60	
7502	Office Stationery	2.49	
7503	Books etc.	4.00	
7550	Telephone	593.87	
8205	Refreshments	3.65	
8207	General expenses	1,855.64	
	Totals:	51,747.48	51,747.48

KAPLAN PUBLISHING

Journals, bad debts and wages 12

CONTENTS

1   Introduction
2   Correction of errors
3   Bad debts
4   Wages

1 Introduction

So far you have learnt how to process day-to-day transactions through SAGE. These have included making sales and purchases and making and receiving payments.

Sometimes, however, a business will need to record an accounting transaction that falls outside the 'norm'. In these instances, a *journal* is required.

Common reasons for journals

- Correction of errors – for example, amending opening balances, removing duplicate entries, or correcting given, or your own, errors

- Writing off bad debts

- Year-end adjustments (e.g. depreciation, accruals and prepayments, closing stock): these are covered at Level III of your ICB studies.

2 Correction of errors

You may find that you enter a transaction incorrectly, and post it to SAGE before you have noticed. In this instance you will need to correct the error by producing a reversing journal.

Earlier, you entered a payment from the bank for £35.00 to Pickerton Darts Association for advertising in their handbook.

It has now come to light that in fact the payment should have been for £55.00, the error being due to misreading the League Secretary's rather poor handwriting on the invoice. The correct amount was in fact paid – reference to the cheque stub and the bank statement would confirm this.

The problem

At the moment, the bank balance is overstated by £20, as we have only entered £35 instead of the correct amount of £55. Also, the expenditure on advertising is understated by the same £20.

The solution

You need to produce a journal to correct this error.

From the **Company** module select the Journal Entry icon.

Enter the details as below:

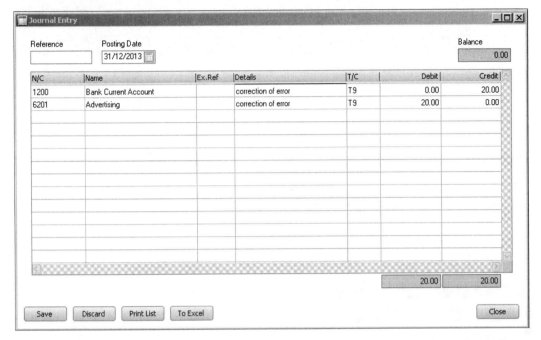

Note the double-entry:

You have credited the bank account by £20 and debited the advertising account by the same amount. Press SAVE.

The corrections function

SAGE also has an in-built corrections function which may be used instead of the more 'traditional' use of the journal. This function can be accessed

via the left-hand pane on the screen by selecting [Corrections] or via the following route:

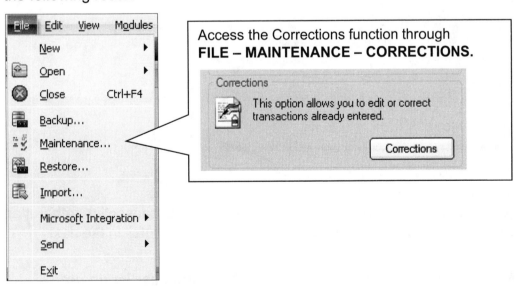

The Corrections function will allow you to correct certain types of errors.

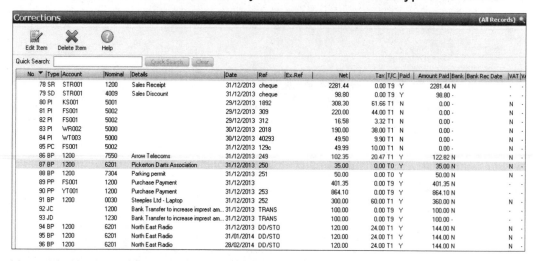

Here, the entry with an error is highlighted. Double click on this:

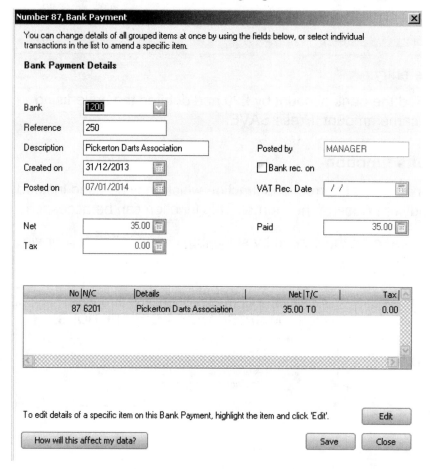

Now you can correct any errors through the original transaction rather than by using a journal. This method is shown in greater detail in the next chapter.

Note: **If you completed the correction by journal earlier do not complete and save the correction through this screen as well.**

3   Bad debts

A bad debt arises when a debtor fails to make payment on their debt to us. At some point the organisation will need to judge that the debt is no longer likely to be recovered and will need to write off the debt. This has the effect of decreasing the total debtors (the sales ledger control account) and creating a bad debt expense that will reduce profits.

To write off a bad debt in SAGE v19 you will need to issue a credit to that particular customer for the amount being written off: this is done by using the Customer Write offs/Refunds wizard in the Customers module. The debit entry for this will be the expense account 'Bad Debts Written Off' (already established in SAGE as N/C 8100). This will ensure that the cost of the bad debt is written off against your profits for the current year.

Bad debts and VAT

When a customer purchases goods or services on credit, the supplier will generally charge them VAT on that supply (assuming of course that they are VAT registered and the supplies attract VAT). If the customer subsequently fails to pay for these items it would be unfair if the supplier continued to bear the cost of the VAT. Rules exist therefore to protect the supplier in this case. The VAT can be reclaimed (i.e. offset against a future VAT liability) so long as the following criteria are met:

The debt is at least six months old.

Genuine attempts have been made to recover the debt.

The debt has been written off in the accounts.

Wynn Bowlden is currently showing Roland Garros (A/c Ref GAR001) as a debtor. The opening balance on this debt relates to coaching sessions almost a year ago, the payment of which has been in dispute with the customer since that time. On 31st December 2013 Wynn Bowlden decided that it was unlikely the issue would ever be resolved and so decided to write the debt off. The amount is £301.28 (including VAT of £50.21).

This is processed as follows:

From within the **CUSTOMERS** module, click the **Customer Write Off/Refunds** button in the Tasks Bar. Highlight **Write off Customer Transactions** as shown below, and then click **Next**.

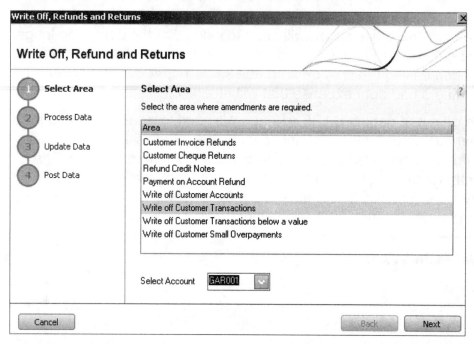

Follow the instructions and select the correct invoice to be written off, as below:

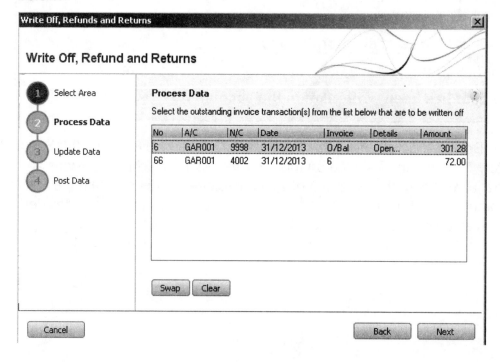

Add a reference and then complete the write-off as instructed:

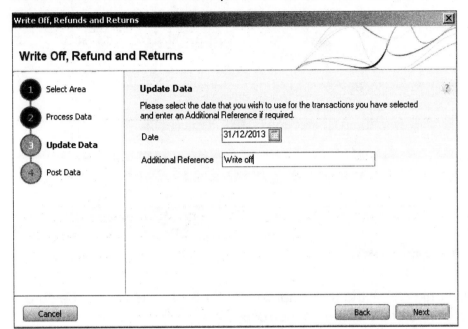

The wizard will write off the debt to N/C8100, **inclusive** of VAT.

If the business meets the criteria for claiming bad debt relief, as explained above, then a further journal entry is required. This journal will transfer the VAT that can be reclaimed from HMRC from N/C8100 Bad debt write off to N/C2201 Purchase tax control account, meaning that the bad debt expense shown in the accounts is then exclusive of VAT.

Here we are told that the VAT on the amount being written off re Roland Garros does meet the criteria for bad debt relief, and amounts to £50.21.

The journal shown below should be entered so that Wynn Bowlden can claim bad debt relief in respect of this balance.

Note that you will need to use the tax code of T1 for the journal entry to N/C2201 so that the bad debt relief is picked up on the VAT return. The tax code of T9 can be used for the corresponding entry to N/C8100.

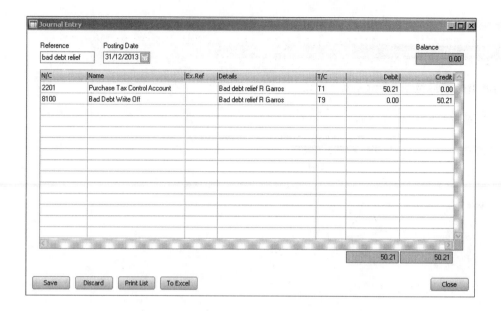

Now you should check the customer record for Roland Garros to be sure that the debt has been written off correctly.

4 Wages

When a company employs someone they (generally) must run a PAYE scheme. This is where the company deducts the employee's tax and national insurance from them and pays it over to HM Revenue and Customs so at the end of the tax year the employee does not have any tax to pay. The wages expense is the debit side of the transaction and the credit side is split into three liabilities: one for the net wages owing to the employee, one for the National Insurance the company now owes HM Revenue and Customs and one for the amount of PAYE the company now owes HM Revenue and Customs.

Depending on how much the employee is paid, it is likely the company will have to make Employer's contributions for National Insurance. You do not need to know the actual rules for this but this is an expense on top of the gross amount of the employee's wages. This will be given on the payroll reports.

Finally there may be other deductions from the employee's wages that the company has to deduct from the wages and pay over. These can include pension payments, attachment of earnings orders and Give As You Earn (GAYE) charitable contributions.

In this scenario we will enter the wages for Wynn Bowlden for December 2013. The expense has been incurred in this month; however Wynn Bowlden does not pay wages until the 5th of the following month.

Assume the wages bill is made up as follows:

Gross Wages £1000

Made up of:
Net Wages £720

Pension Contributions £60

PAYE £140

National Insurance £180

Employers' NI Contributions £100

You need to post the following journal:

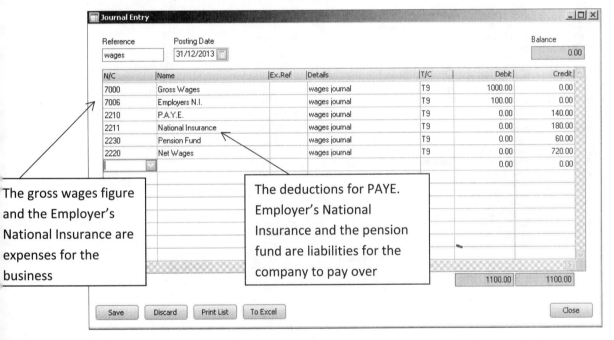

The gross wages figure and the Employer's National Insurance are expenses for the business

The deductions for PAYE. Employer's National Insurance and the pension fund are liabilities for the company to pay over

Now print off a trial balance for the year ended 31st December 2013 and make sure your balances agree to the ones shown below.

Wynn Bowlden Tennis Coach
Period Trial Balance

Page: 1

To Period: Month 12, December 2013

N/C	Name	Debit	Credit
0030	Office Equipment	3,720.00	
0031	Office Equipment Depreciation		1,710.00
0050	Motor Vehicles	8,000.00	
0051	Motor Vehicles Depreciation		2,000.00
1001	Stock	2,865.90	
1100	Debtors Control Account	2,714.33	
1200	Bank Current Account	14,421.26	
1230	Petty Cash	200.00	
1235	Cash Register	195.56	
2100	Creditors Control Account		3,827.90
2200	Sales Tax Control Account		676.11
2201	Purchase Tax Control Account	302.06	
2202	VAT Liability		981.61
2210	P.A.Y.E.		140.00
2211	National Insurance		180.00
2220	Net Wages		720.00
2230	Pension Fund		60.00
3000	Capital		3,500.00
3200	Profit and Loss Account		4,121.14
4000	Sales - Equipment		4,565.53
4001	Sales - Clothing and Footwear		2,283.79
4002	Sales - Individual Coaching		13,469.30
4003	Sales - Group Coaching		13,910.50
4004	Sales - Other		601.60
4009	Discounts Allowed	38.80	
4200	Sales of Assets		100.00
5000	Purchases - Equipment	1,254.70	
5001	Purchases- Clothing and Footwear	1,618.90	
5002	Purchases - Stationery	601.79	
5003	Purchases - Packaging	208.78	
5004	Purchases - Other consumables	104.61	
6201	Advertising	175.00	
7000	Gross Wages	1,000.00	
7006	Employers N.I.	100.00	
7100	Rent	3,600.00	
7103	General Rates	350.00	
7304	Miscellaneous Motor Expenses	8,654.47	
7400	Travelling	5.00	
7501	Postage and Carriage	5.60	
7502	Office Stationery	2.49	
7503	Books etc.	4.00	
7550	Telephone	593.87	
8100	Bad Debt Write Off	251.07	
8205	Refreshments	3.65	
8207	General expenses	1,855.64	
	Totals:	**52,847.48**	**52,847.48**

Amending company details and managing data

CONTENTS

1 Amending data

As we have already seen, one of the most common ways to correct an error is by means of a journal. This is essentially a book-keeping solution, using a double entry to correct or amend an earlier error. Sometimes, however, it is necessary to change a transaction we have entered that we cannot correct with a journal.

For example, in the Wynn Bowlden Case Study we entered a credit note for Annette Chord (A/c ref CHO001) for a cancelled coaching session. We cannot enter a journal to correct this as Sage does not allow us to post a journal to an individual sales (or purchase) ledger account. If we needed to correct this simply access the Corrections screen from the Tasks menu

Corrections

Within the Corrections function we have the choice of searching for the item we are trying to correct by many different criteria. One good way to do this is to use the account reference.

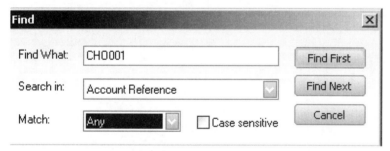

By searching by the account reference of the transaction we are trying to find we can search through the transactions until we find the one we want by clicking ⌗Find Next⌗ .

Once we have found the transaction we want we have the choice of either deleting or amending the transaction by clicking the buttons at the top of the screen.

Pressing delete brings up the following screen:

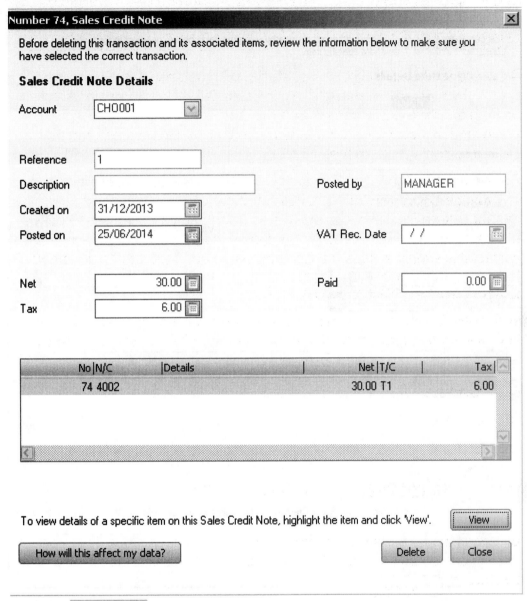

Clicking [Delete] will delete the transaction from the ledger although the fact that it existed will always be shown and it will be offset by a deleting entry as opposed to being completely removed from the ledgers.

Pressing edit brings up the following screen:

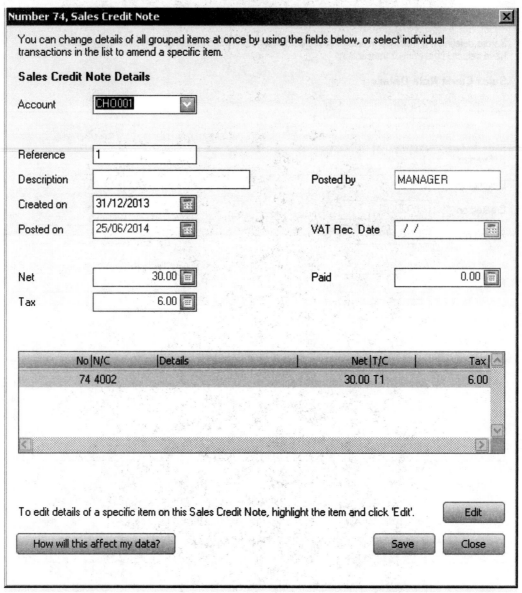

You can amend the details of the credit note from this screen such as the account, description or date of the transaction, the nominal code, details, net amount, VAT amount and tax code.

Further information on correcting entries can be found through the SAGE help facility.

File   Edit   View   Modules   Settings   Tools   WebLinks   News Feeds   Help

2 Exporting data

You may wish to export data from SAGE to another program – for example, a spreadsheet.

Let us imagine that you want to export details of the company's credit suppliers to Microsoft Excel.

Bring up the supplier list screen as required and then simply click **on FILE – MICROSOFT INTEGRATION – CONTENTS TO MICROSOFT EXCEL** (or whichever program you want to export to).

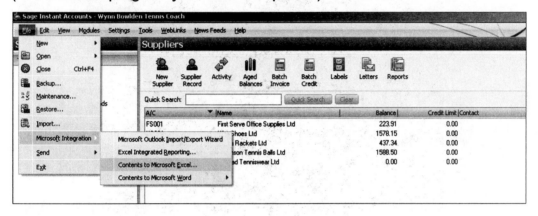

This will export the data to your spreadsheet as below:

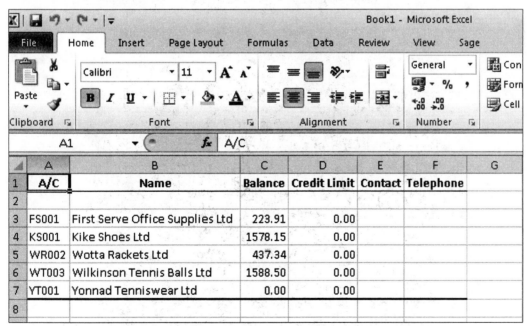

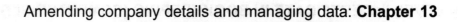

Health and safety

CONTENTS

1 Introduction

For your assessment, you may need to display an awareness of health and safety issues when using a computer system.

2 Risks of using a computerised system

Computerised accounting systems may offer a lot of advantages to businesses, but organisations must also be aware of the potential risks posed by such systems. These risks can be categorised as:

- **Physical risks** – caused by system failure, theft, damage or loss or corruption of data, and access to systems or data by unauthorised users

- **Virus threats** – the risk of a computer virus (or similar) being introduced to a network, with the resultant loss of or damage to data

- **Legal threats** – from contravention of legislation such as the Data Protection Act (1998) by an organisation in the way that it stores or uses personal data.

Accounting data is particularly at risk, because it is highly confidential and potentially highly valuable to other people. Hence you must remain especially vigilant to risks to data security.

Types of risk

Physical Risks

Risk	Possible Safeguards
Damage from spillage (e.g. liquid)	• No food or drink permitted near computer workstations
Electrical connections becoming worn or damaged	• Keep workstations and desks tidy, with all cabling carefully and tidily arranged • Avoid overloading circuits by plugging too many plugs into a socket or adaptor • Carry out regular visual checks for frayed cables, exposed wires etc. Report any incidences that you find
Theft of computer hardware	• Hardware may be fastened to desks etc. (although it may still be possible to open the casing to remove hard drives) • Regular physical checks of IT equipment to ensure the actual equipment matches that held on the Fixed Asset Register • Use of bar-codes and other identifying details to ensure that any items stolen can be quickly returned if found
Damage to, or loss of, memory devices (e.g. CDs, USB pen drives)	• Treat all storage devices with care. Although modern devices are quite durable, they can still be scratched or damaged. Even grease left by fingerprints can damage the effectiveness of the disk. • Avoid exposure to devices which contain large magnets – this can corrupt data on the storage device

	• Be extremely vigilant if you are taking memory devices with you out of the office – to work at home or on the train, for example. There are many examples of instances where highly confidential data has been lost in this way. Remember, the data on the CD/USB pen drive is usually far more valuable than the device itself
	• Take regular backups of data which are named appropriately and stored off-site in secure storage or online using a secure cloud service.
'Prying eyes' – unauthorised viewing of confidential information by colleagues, clients or others	• Remember, if you can see confidential information on your computer screen, others may be able to as well. Angle your screen and arrange your workspace to minimise the risk of other people seeing your work.
	• Always log out of a program if you are leaving your desk
	• Do not leave confidential papers on your desk. Be especially wary if there are people other than colleagues in your office
	• Use a password to protect access to your computer, and make sure that the program automatically logs you out after a few minutes of inactivity

Virus threats

All computers that are linked to 'the outside world' (e.g. via a network or to the internet) are susceptible to security threats. Many people are familiar with the threat posed by viruses or other similar threats.

A virus is a piece of software that is used to maliciously infect your computer. What is more, it then has the ability to replicate itself and infect any other computer that is connected to yours. Of course, this also means that your computer is at risk of being infected by other computers as well.

Introduction of the virus to a system usually takes place when you open a file that has been deliberately infected – for example, an email attachment or a web-site, an infected piece of software, or an infected memory device (e.g. a memory stick).

The consequences of being infected by a virus are many:

- Infecting all other computers you are linked to

- Deleting particular files – especially files which are essential to the normal operation of your computer

- Altering files so they are no longer legible

- Slowing down your computer by taking up huge amounts of memory – leaving your computer extremely slow and unable to perform basic tasks

- Accessing your data and sending it to other people

- 'Reading' your passwords for essential sites such as on-line banking – enabling somebody else to access your bank account

- Wiping your hard-drive – essentially deleting everything from the computer.

Safeguards against viruses

Firewalls: These are designed to prevent 'hackers' gaining access to a computer network via the internet or a network. These can be a piece of software (now often built in to operating systems such as Windows) or a hardware firewall, which is essentially the router or a network box which acts as a barrier between the modem (the phone line into your computer) and the computer itself. An effective firewall is an essential aspect of computer safeguarding, particularly where users have access to the internet.

Effective IT policies: Most organisations now have clearly defined IT policies regarding the private use of the internet and e-mails, not allowing employees to install their own software (e.g. games) on work computers.

Using virus protection software: This is the most important method of protecting computer systems. It acts as a guard dog, constantly watching for suspicious files, blocking or destroying them and advising the user that there has been an attempt to compromise the security of the system. As virus protection programs are constantly being updated with details of new viruses, it is essential that it is kept updated and current at all times. An out-of-date program is no protection against the most recent viruses.

Personal vigilance: Be very wary if you receive unsolicited emails from addresses that you do not recognise. Do not open any emails that you are suspicious of – you should report these to your IT manager or your supervisor. However, you should also be wary of emails (particularly those with attachments) from addresses you <u>do</u> recognise – remember, if somebody you know has a computer which has been infected there is a high probability that the computer will then try and attack your computer as well.

Be very careful when accessing the internet. Only use sites you need for work. Be wary of links to other sites that you do not recognise. Again, if you are in any doubt, or suspect that your computer may have been the victim of a virus, inform your supervisor.

Passwords

Passwords are one of the most common – and most abused – forms of computer security. In most businesses the access to each computer is protected by a password, as well as access to different pieces of software. Even individual files and documents can and should be protected if they contain confidential or sensitive information.

The choice of password is very important: you should be able to remember it, but it should not be easily guessed by others. Ideally, a password should:

- Be at least 6-8 characters long.
- Contain a mixture of upper and lower case letters and numbers.
- Not be a recognisable word.

Under no circumstances should you choose something like your own name, you child's name or your pet dog's name – these are far too easy for someone with only a small amount of knowledge about you to guess. You should also avoid obvious combinations such as 'password' or '123456'.

You should be able to remember your own password. Do not be tempted to write it down in your diary, on a scrap of paper in your top drawer, or even on a sticky note and attach it to the monitor!

You should also never tell anybody else your password – even your most trusted colleague. If you do suspect that somebody knows what your password is, you should change it immediately.

Many systems are configured to require you to change your password every few weeks – even if yours is not, this is good practice.

Backups

Occasionally data is lost, whether through an unforeseen circumstance such as a fire or through computer failure. It is therefore essential that organisations take appropriate steps to minimise the risk of data loss, and to minimise the impact of data loss if it does happen.

Backups should be taken on a regular basis, and at least once a day in most businesses. In addition, individual files should regularly be backed up whilst working on them. There is little more frustrating than spending an hour producing a document or a spreadsheet only to lose it and not to have a backup.

Many programs (including Microsoft Office applications) have an auto-recovery function – essentially a backup is taken automatically every few minutes without the user having to do anything. If there is an interruption or failure (e.g. a power cut) only a small amount of work would be lost, and the affected file can very quickly and easily be recovered.

Copies of backups should be kept securely to prevent unauthorised access or accidental damage. It is good practice to keep a backup at a secondary location (i.e. off site or online). This way, if there is a fire or a burglary the backup data will not be destroyed or stolen. Some businesses may still take physical backups off site (such as a CD), but this increases the risk of that back up being lost or stolen while away from the office. It is becoming increasingly common for organisations to pay an IT company to keep remote backups electronically or to use a reliable cloud storage provider.

The Data Protection Act (1998)

The Data Protection Act (DPA) is designed to protect the rights of the individual whose personal data is held and used by other people or organisations.

Personal data are defined in the DPA as:

"data which relate to a living individual who can be identified:

- from those data or

- from those data and other information which is in the possession of, or likely to come into the possession of, the *data controller* and includes any expression of opinion about the individual and any indication of the intentions of the data controller or any other person in respect of the individual"

The data controller is a person who determines the purposes for which and the manner in which any personal data are, or are to be, processed.

 Example

If you have enrolled at a local college or training provider for a bookkeeping course, you will have been required to complete an enrolment form. The information you will have completed on the enrolment form is likely to have included your name, gender, ethnicity, birthday, address, national insurance number, your qualifications, any health issues you may have, your bank details and so on. It is essential for the college or training provider to have this very personal and confidential information about you to process your application, to secure possible funding and to send you an invoice or set up a direct debit for your course fees.

However, you may then raise the question – what happens to all this information once my application has been processed? How long does the organisation keep the data about me? What else is it used for? Is it sold to any external bodies (e.g. for marketing purposes)?

These questions (and more) are addressed by the Data Protection Act.

The Data Protection Act has **EIGHT PRINCIPLES**, which state that personal data must be:

1 Processed fairly and lawfully

2 Obtained for specified and lawful purposes

3 Adequate, relevant and not excessive

4 Accurate and up-to-date

5   Not kept any longer than necessary

6   Processed in accordance with the data subject's (i.e. the individual's) rights

7   Securely kept

8   Not transferred to any other country without adequate protection in situ.

Individuals have a number of rights:

- To be informed of all of the information held about them by an organisation

- To prevent the processing of their data for the purposes of direct marketing

- To compensation if they can show that a contravention of the DPA has led to loss or damage

- To have inaccurate data removed or corrected

If the data held by an organisation is *sensitive* then extra safeguards must be put in place. Sensitive data is defined by the act as data pertaining to:

- Racial or ethnic origin

- Religious or similar beliefs

- Trade union membership

- Physical or mental health or sexual life

- Political opinions

- Criminal offences

Data about one or more of these sensitive issues may only be held in strictly defined situations or where explicit consent has been obtained.

You can find out more about the Data Protection Act at

www.ico.gov.uk/for_organisations/data_protection.aspx

Protecting yourself whilst using the computer

In addition to protecting your computer and your data, you should also take care to protect yourself. You should make sure that you follow these guidelines on safe working:

- Make sure that your workstation and chair are correctly set up. The screen should be level with your eyes to aid your posture, whilst your chair should be comfortable and support your back. A well-designed workstation and chair can minimise the risk of issues such as wrist injuries and back and neck problems

- Do not sit in the same position for too long. You should aim to take short frequent breaks if you are working at the computer for any length of time – as a guideline you should consider a 5-10 minute break every hour or so.

- Keep your work safe clear and tidy; be organised and ensure you file papers away safely when you have finished using them.

- Do not have drinks or food near your workstation – accidental spillages can easily happen and can have significant consequences!

- There are no proven links between using a VDU (Visual Display Unit) and damage to eyesight, but if you feel that your eyesight is worsening, or you suffer from headaches, you should consult your optician. If you use a computer screen regularly at work you may be entitled to an eye-test and /or free spectacles, paid for by your employer. If you have an occupational health or human resources department at work they will provide you with more information.

Reports

15

CONTENTS

1 Introduction

Although it is possible to create and produce your own SAGE reports, there are a number of extremely useful report layouts already set up.

2 The Audit Trail

One of the most useful reports on Sage is the Audit Trail. This provides you with a full list of all transactions that you have entered. Each transaction is numbered sequentially, with corresponding details such as the date, the type of transaction (e.g. JC = Journal Credit, JD = Journal Debit), any narrative or description you have entered and so on.

To access the Audit Trail enter **COMPANY – FINANCIALS** and then click on the Audit Trail icon.

As with most reports, you can select which level of detail you require (brief, summary, detailed, or deleted transactions), and whether you wish to send the report to the printer, simply to preview it on screen, or to save it.

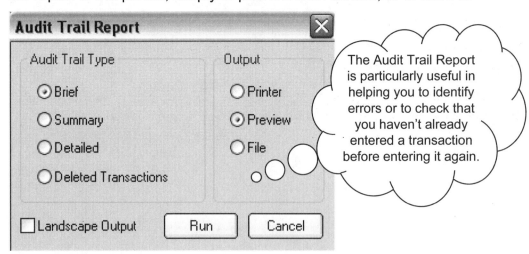

The Audit Trail Report is particularly useful in helping you to identify errors or to check that you haven't already entered a transaction before entering it again.

You can then choose whether to view all transactions, or whether to search by criteria such as date of transaction, transaction number, or by specific suppliers or customers.

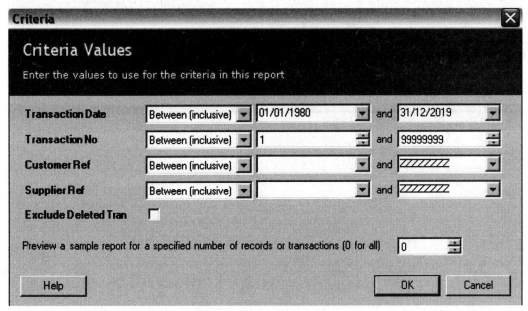

You should note that, as with other areas of Sage, any deleted transactions will be shown in RED.

3 Other reports

You have already seen a number of these throughout this manual.

You should now make yourself familiar with these, plus the other reports shown on the following pages.

Note that there are many other reports within SAGE; you should take the time to examine all of these to find the reports that will best suit your business.

Customer reports

Aged Debtors Analysis

Date: 08/01/2014			**Wynn Bowlden Tennis Coach**					Page: 1
Time: 11:03:14			**Aged Debtors Analysis (Detailed)**					

Date From:	01/01/1980			Customer From:	
Date To:	31/12/2013			Customer To:	ZZZZZZZ
Include future transactions:	No				
Exclude later payments:	No				

** NOTE: All report values are shown in Base Currency, unless otherwise indicated **

A/C:	BAT001	Name:	G Bates		Contact:			Tel:		
No	Type	Date	Ref	Details	Balance	Future	Current	Period 1	Period 2	Period 3	Older
64	SI	31/12/2013	4		144.00	0.00	144.00	0.00	0.00	0.00	0.00
				Totals:	144.00	0.00	144.00	0.00	0.00	0.00	0.00

Turnover: 120.00
Credit Limit £ 0.00

A/C:	CHA001	Name:	Noah Chang		Contact:			Tel:		
No	Type	Date	Ref	Details	Balance	Future	Current	Period 1	Period 2	Period 3	Older
8	SI	31/12/2013	O/Bal	Opening Balance	59.26	0.00	59.26	0.00	0.00	0.00	0.00
61	SI	31/12/2013	1		70.00	0.00	70.00	0.00	0.00	0.00	0.00
				Totals:	129.26	0.00	129.26	0.00	0.00	0.00	0.00

Turnover: 167.59
Credit Limit £ 0.00

A/C:	CHO001	Name:	Annette Chord		Contact:			Tel:		
No	Type	Date	Ref	Details	Balance	Future	Current	Period 1	Period 2	Period 3	Older
10	SI	31/12/2013	O/Bal	Opening Balance	819.20	0.00	819.20	0.00	0.00	0.00	0.00
62	SI	31/12/2013	2		72.00	0.00	72.00	0.00	0.00	0.00	0.00
65	SI	31/12/2013	5		36.00	0.00	36.00	0.00	0.00	0.00	0.00
68	SI	31/12/2013	8		716.40	0.00	716.40	0.00	0.00	0.00	0.00
70	SC	31/12/2013	1		-36.00	0.00	-36.00	0.00	0.00	0.00	0.00
				Totals:	1,607.60	0.00	1,607.60	0.00	0.00	0.00	0.00

Turnover: 1,479.20
Credit Limit £ 0.00

Shows a list of debtors with analysis of how long the debts have been in existence. **Note:** The screenshot above is only an extract of the report.

Day Books – Customer Invoices

Date: 26/06/2014		**Wynn Bowlden Tennis Coach**		Page: 1
Time: 13:12:43		**Day Books: Customer Invoices (Summary)**		

Date From:	01/01/1980			Customer From:	
Date To:	31/12/2019			Customer To:	ZZZZZZZ

Transaction	1
Transaction To:	99,999,999

Tran No.	Items	Tp	Date	A/C Ref	Inv Ref	Details	Net Amount	Tax Amount	Gross Amount
6	1	SI	31/12/2013	GAR001	O/Bal	Opening Balance	301.28	0.00	301.28
7	1	SI	31/12/2013	RAN002	O/Bal	Opening Balance	1,820.49	0.00	1,820.49
8	1	SI	31/12/2013	CHA001	O/Bal	Opening Balance	109.26	0.00	109.26
9	1	SI	31/12/2013	LIT001	O/Bal	Opening Balance	209.47	0.00	209.47
10	1	SI	31/12/2013	CHO001	O/Bal	Opening Balance	819.20	0.00	819.20
65	1	SI	31/12/2013	CHA001	1		58.33	11.67	70.00
66	1	SI	31/12/2013	CHO001	2		60.00	12.00	72.00
67	1	SI	31/12/2013	LIT001	3		220.00	44.00	264.00
68	1	SI	31/12/2013	BAT001	4		120.00	24.00	144.00
69	1	SI	31/12/2013	CHO001	5		30.00	6.00	36.00
70	1	SI	31/12/2013	GAR001	6		60.00	12.00	72.00
71	1	SI	31/12/2013	RAN002	7		240.00	48.00	288.00
72	1	SI	31/12/2013	CHO001	8		600.00	116.40	716.40
73	1	SI	31/12/2013	STR001	9		1,940.00	380.24	2,320.24
						Totals:	6,588.03	654.31	7,242.34

Shows a list of all sales invoices produced inc. the Net, VAT and Gross Amounts.

Customer Activity - Detailed

Date: 08/01/2014
Time: 11:15:19

Wynn Bowlden Tennis Coach
Customer Activity (Detailed)

Page: 1

Date From:	01/01/1980	
Date To:	31/12/2013	
Transaction From:	1	
Transaction To:	99,999,999	
Inc b/fwd transaction:	No	
Exc later payment:	No	

Customer From:		
Customer To:	ZZZZZZZ	
N/C From:		
N/C To:	99999999	
Dept From:	0	
Dept To:	999	

** NOTE: All report values are shown in Base Currency, unless otherwise indicated **

A/C: BAT001   **Name:**   G Bates   **Contact:**   **Tel:**

No	Type	Date	Ref	N/C	Details	Dept	T/C	Value	O/S	Debit	Credit	V	B
64	SI	31/12/2013	4	4002		0	T1	144.00 *	144.00	144.00		N	-
							Totals:	144.00	144.00	144.00			

Amount Outstanding	144.00
Amount Paid this period	0.00
Credit Limit £	0.00
Turnover YTD	120.00

A/C: CHA001   **Name:**   Noah Chang   **Contact:**   **Tel:**

No	Type	Date	Ref	N/C	Details	Dept	T/C	Value	O/S	Debit	Credit	V	B
8	SI	31/12/2013	O/Bal	9998	Opening Balance	0	T9	109.26 p	59.26	109.26		-	-
61	SI	31/12/2013	1	4001		0	T1	70.00 *	70.00	70.00		N	-
75	SR	31/12/2013	cash	1235	Sales Receipt	0	T9	50.00			50.00	-	-
							Totals:	129.26	129.26	179.26	50.00		

Amount Outstanding	129.26
Amount Paid this period	50.00

Shows all transactions for customers (e.g. sales and receipts).

Supplier reports

Aged Creditors Analysis

Date: 08/01/2014
Time: 11:17:36

Wynn Bowlden Tennis Coach
Aged Creditors Analysis (Detailed)

Page: 1

Date From:	01/01/1980	
Date To:	31/12/2013	
Include future transactions:	No	
Exclude later payments:	No	

Supplier From:	
Supplier To:	ZZZZZZZ

** NOTE: All report values are shown in Base Currency, unless otherwise indicated **

A/C: FS001   **Name:**   First Serve Office Supplies Ltd   **Contact:**   **Tel:**

No:	Type	Date	Ref	Details	Balance	Future	Current	Period 1	Period 2	Period 3	Older
81	PI	29/12/2013	309		264.00	0.00	264.00	0.00	0.00	0.00	0.00
82	PI	29/12/2013	312		19.90	0.00	19.90	0.00	0.00	0.00	0.00
85	PC	31/12/2013	129c		-59.99	0.00	-59.99	0.00	0.00	0.00	0.00
				Totals:	223.91	0.00	223.91	0.00	0.00	0.00	0.00

Turnover:	587.94
Credit Limit £	0.00

A/C: KS001   **Name:**   Kike Shoes Ltd   **Contact:**   **Tel:**

No:	Type	Date	Ref	Details	Balance	Future	Current	Period 1	Period 2	Period 3	Older
2	PI	31/12/2013	O/Bal	Opening Balance	1,208.19	0.00	1,208.19	0.00	0.00	0.00	0.00
80	PI	29/12/2013	1892		369.96	0.00	369.96	0.00	0.00	0.00	0.00
				Totals:	1,578.15	0.00	1,578.15	0.00	0.00	0.00	0.00

Turnover:	1,516.49
Credit Limit £	0.00

Shows the outstanding creditor balances and how long the debts have been in existence. **Note this is only an extract of the whole report.**

Supplier Activity Report

| Date: 08/01/2014 | | **Wynn Bowlden Tennis Coach** | | | Page: 1 |
| Time: 11:19:17 | | **Supplier Activity (Detailed)** | | | |

Date From:	01/01/1980		**Supplier From:**	
Date To:	31/12/2013		**Supplier To:**	ZZZZZZZZ
Transaction From:	1		**N/C From:**	
Transaction To:	99,999,999		**N/C To:**	99999999
Inc b/fwd transaction:	No		**Dept From:**	0
Exc later payment:	No		**Dept To:**	999

** NOTE: All report values are shown in Base Currency, unless otherwise indicated **

A/C: FS001   **Name:** First Serve Office Supplies Ltd   **Contact:**   **Tel:**

No	Type	Date	Ref	N/C	Details	Dept	T/C	Value	O/S	Debit	Credit	V	B
5	PI	31/12/2013	O/Bal	9998	Opening Balance	0	T9	401.35	0.00		401.35	-	-
81	PI	29/12/2013	309	5002		0	T1	264.00 *	264.00		264.00	N	-
82	PI	29/12/2013	312	5002		0	T1	19.90 *	19.90		19.90	N	-
85	PC	31/12/2013	129c	5002		0	T1	59.99 *	-59.99	59.99		N	-
89	PP	31/12/2013		1200	Purchase Payment	0	T9	401.35	0.00	401.35		-	N
					Totals:			223.91	223.91	461.34	685.25		

Amount Outstanding	223.91
Amount paid this period	401.35
Credit Limit £	0.00
Turnover YTD	587.94

Shows all transactions for a single, or range of, suppliers, including purchases, returns, payments etc. **Again, note only an extract is shown here.**

Supplier Invoices Due

| Date: 08/01/2014 | | **Wynn Bowlden Tennis Coach** | | Page: 1 |
| Time: 11:20:08 | | **Supplier Invoices Due** | | |

Supplier From:			**Date From:**	01/01/1980
Supplier To:	ZZZZZZZZ		**Date To:**	31/12/2013
Transaction From:	1		**Exc Later Payments:**	No
Transaction To:	99,999,999			

A/C: FS001   **Name:** First Serve Office Supplies Ltd   **Contact:**   **Tel:**

No	Type	Ref	Date	Details	Amount	Paid	Outstanding
81	PI	309	29/12/2013		264.00	0.00	264.00
82	PI	312	29/12/2013		19.90	0.00	19.90
85	PC	129c	31/12/2013		59.99	0.00	-59.99
				Total:			223.91

A/C: KS001   **Name:** Kike Shoes Ltd   **Contact:**   **Tel:**

No	Type	Ref	Date	Details	Amount	Paid	Outstanding
2	PI	O/Bal	31/12/2013	Opening Balance	1,208.19	0.00	1,208.19
80	PI	1892	29/12/2013		369.96	0.00	369.96
				Total:			1,578.15

Shows the list of all invoices due to be paid. **Only an extract is shown here.**

Top Supplier List

| Date: | 08/01/2014 | | **Wynn Bowlden Tennis Coach** | | | Page: | 1 |
| Time: | 11:20:59 | | **Top Supplier List - YTD** | | | | |

** NOTE: All report values are shown in Base Currency, unless otherwise indicated **

Account Ref	Name	Telephone	Contact Name	Last Inv Date	Credit Limit	Turnover YTD
WT003	Wilkinson Tennis Balls Ltd			30/12/2013	£ 0.00	1,578.60
KS001	Kike Shoes Ltd			29/12/2013	£ 0.00	1,516.49
YT001	Yonnad Tenniswear Ltd			31/12/2013	£ 0.00	864.10
FS001	First Serve Office Supplies Ltd			29/12/2013	£ 0.00	587.94
WR002	Wotta Rackets Ltd			30/12/2013	£ 0.00	399.34

Shows a list of suppliers in order of value of purchases from them.

Bank reports

Day Books: Bank Payments

| Date: 08/01/2014 | | | **Wynn Bowlden Tennis Coach** | | | | Page: 1 |
| Time: 11:22:46 | | | **Day Books: Bank Payments (Detailed)** | | | | |

Date From:	01/01/1980					Bank From:	1200
Date To:	31/12/2019					Bank To:	1200
Transaction From:	1					N/C From:	
Transaction To:	99,999,999					N/C To:	99999999
Dept From:	0						
Dept To:	999						

Bank: 1200   Currency: Pound Sterling

No	Type	N/C	Date	Ref	Details	Dept	Net £	Tax £	T/C	Gross£	V	B	Bank Rec. Date
86	BP	7550	31/12/2013	249	Arrow Telecoms	0	102.35	20.47	T1	122.82	N	N	
87	BP	6201	31/12/2013	250	Pickerton Darts	0	35.00	0.00	T0	35.00	N	N	
88	BP	7304	31/12/2013	251	Parking permit	0	50.00	0.00	T0	50.00	N	N	
91	BP	0030	31/12/2013	252	Steeples Ltd -	0	300.00	60.00	T1	360.00	N	N	
94	BP	6201	31/12/2013	DD/STO	North East Radio	0	120.00	24.00	T1	144.00	N	N	
95	BP	6201	31/01/2014	DD/STO	North East Radio	0	120.00	24.00	T1	144.00	N	N	
96	BP	6201	28/02/2014	DD/STO	North East Radio	0	120.00	24.00	T1	144.00	N	N	
97	BP	6201	31/03/2014	DD/STO	North East Radio	0	120.00	24.00	T1	144.00	N	N	
					Totals £		967.35	176.47		1,143.82			

Shows all payments from the chosen bank account.

Similar reports are available for cash and credit card payments and receipts.

Day Books: Customer Receipts

Date: 08/01/2014				**Wynn Bowlden Tennis Coach**						**Page:** 1	
Time: 11:24:32				**Day Books: Customer Receipts (Detailed)**							

Date From: 01/01/1980						**Bank From:**	1200
Date To: 31/12/2019						**Bank To:**	1200
Transaction From: 1						**Customer From:**	
Transaction To: 99,999,999						**Customer To:**	ZZZZZZZ

Bank: 1200   **Currency:** Pound Sterling

No	Type	A/C	Date	Ref	Details	Net £	Tax £	T/C	Gross £	V	B	Bank Rec. Date
74	SR	RAN002	31/12/2013	cheque	Sales Receipt	1,820.49	0.00	T9	1,820.49	-	N	
			- 31/12/2013	O/Bal	1820.49 to SI 7							
78	SR	STR001	31/12/2013	cheque	Sales Receipt	2,281.44	0.00	T9	2,281.44	-	N	
			- 31/12/2013	9	2281.44 to SI 69							
					Totals £	4,101.93	0.00		4,101.93			

Shows all customer receipts

Day Book: Supplier Payments

Date: 08/01/2014				**Wynn Bowlden Tennis Coach**						**Page:** 1	
Time: 11:25:56				**Day Books: Supplier Payments (Detailed)**							

Date From: 01/01/1980						**Bank From:**	1200
DateTo: 31/12/2019						**Bank To:**	1200
Transaction From: 1						**Supplier From:**	
Transaction To: 99,999,999						**Supplier To:**	ZZZZZZZ

Bank 1200   **Currency** Pound Sterling

No	Type	A/C	Date	Ref	Details	Net £	Tax £	T/C	Gross £	V	B	Bank Rec Date
89	PP	FS001	31/12/2013		Purchase Payment	401.35	0.00	T9	401.35	-	N	
			- 31/12/2013	O/Bal	401.35 to PI 5							
90	PP	YT001	31/12/2013	253	Purchase Payment	864.10	0.00	T9	864.10	-	N	
			- 31/12/2013	O/Bal	864.10 to PI 1							
					Totals £	1,265.45	0.00		1,265.45			

Shows all payments made to suppliers

Nominal reports

Nominal List

Date:	08/01/2014	**Wynn Bowlden Tennis Coach**	Page:	1
Time:	11:28:01	**Nominal List**		

N/C From:
N/C To: 99999999

N/C	Name
0010	Freehold Property
0011	Leasehold Property
0020	Plant and Machinery
0021	Plant/Machinery Depreciation
0030	Office Equipment
0031	Office Equipment Depreciation
0040	Furniture and Fixtures
0041	Furniture/Fixture Depreciation
0050	Motor Vehicles
0051	Motor Vehicles Depreciation
1001	Stock
1002	Work in Progress
1003	Finished Goods
1004	Raw Materials
1100	Debtors Control Account
1101	Sundry Debtors
1102	Other Debtors
1103	Prepayments
1104	Inter-company Debtors
1105	Provision for credit notes

Shows all nominal codes. **Only an extract is shown here.**

Nominal Activity

Date:	08/01/2014	**Wynn Bowlden Tennis Coach**	Page:	1
Time:	11:32:11	**Nominal Activity – Excluding No Transactions**		

Date From:	01/01/1980	N/C From:	
Date To:	31/12/2013	N/C To:	99999999

Transaction From:	1
Transaction To:	99,999,999

| N/C: | 0030 | Name: | Office Equipment | | | | | Account Balance: | | 3,720.00 DR |

No	Type	Date	Account	Ref	Details	Dept	T/C	Value	Debit	Credit	V	B
15	JD	31/12/2013	0030	O/Bal	Opening Balance	0	T9	3,420.00	3,420.00		-	-
91	BP	31/12/2013	1200	252	Steeples Ltd - Laptop	0	T1	300.00	300.00		N	N
							Totals:		3,720.00			
							History Balance:		3,720.00			

| N/C: | 0031 | Name: | Office Equipment Depreciation | | | | | Account Balance: | | 1,710.00 CR |

No	Type	Date	Account	Ref	Details	Dept	T/C	Value	Debit	Credit	V	B
17	JC	31/12/2013	0031	O/Bal	Opening Balance	0	T9	1,710.00		1,710.00	-	-
							Totals:			1,710.00		
							History Balance:			1,710.00		

| N/C: | 0050 | Name: | Motor Vehicles | | | | | Account Balance: | | 8,000.00 DR |

No	Type	Date	Account	Ref	Details	Dept	T/C	Value	Debit	Credit	V	B
11	JD	31/12/2013	0050	O/Bal	Opening Balance	0	T9	8,000.00	8,000.00		-	-
							Totals:		8,000.00			

Shows all activity in the nominal accounts, including journals: a range of accounts and transaction dates can be selected for the report.

Printing reports – *IMPORTANT*

Businesses find it very useful to keep hard-copy (i.e. printed) versions of their reports. They are useful for future reference, for showing to colleagues or managers and, if necessary, to auditors or other external parties.

However, all businesses must also be aware of the following issues of keeping hard copies. Keeping printed reports takes up valuable space; care must be taken to ensure they are kept free from damp and other factors that could damage them. Businesses must also be aware of the confidentiality aspect; by their very nature, financial reports contain very sensitive financial data which should not be disclosed to people who do not have the authority to see them. The more reports there are, the more likely it is that somebody else may see them, and the greater the storage implications – most businesses use lockable, secure cabinets to file confidential information, whilst bigger organisations may need specialist storage facilities.

Then, of course, there is the cost – both financial and environmental. Paper and printing ink cost money, and so businesses should aim to reduce costs wherever possible. There is also a significant environmental impact to paper wastage and ink use. All businesses – and you – should therefore remember the golden rules of printing reports:

1   **Preview first** – all reports on Sage can be previewed on screen before printing. You should always preview first to ensure that the report you are about to print actually provides you with the correct data

2   **Print only what you need** – there is no point printing 70 pages when you only want one small section of the report. Sage allows you to select by a range of criteria and you should get into the habit of carefully selecting your print range before printing

3   **Draft quality except for final reports** – most printers provide a range of settings for the print quality produced – setting your printer to 'draft quality' means printing will take less time and use less ink. Similarly, print in black and white rather than colour, unless it is a final version for presentation to the organisation's management.

4   **Recycle** – don't just throw paper in the bin – make sure it is re-used (if possible) and then recycled. If you are reusing paper (e.g. as scrap) be wary of confidentiality issues

Following these simple rules should:

1   **SAVE PAPER**

2   **SAVE INK**

3   **SAVE THE ENVIRONMENT**

4   **SAVE MONEY**

PRACTICE ASSESSMENT

1 Practice Assessment Questions

Instructions to candidate

This assignment is based on an existing business, The ExeFactory, an organisation that makes and sells a range of microphones and speaker systems which it sells to a range of customers. The owner of the business is Simeon Powell, who operates as a sole trader.

At the start of business Simeon operated a manual book-keeping system, but has now decided that from 1st April 2014 the accounting system will become computerised. You are employed as a part-time bookkeeper in the business.

You can assume that all documentation within this assessment has been checked for accuracy and duly authorised by Simeon.

Sales are to be analysed in three ways:

- *Fun and Funky* – a range of cheap microphones and speaker systems ideal for home karaoke machines etc.

- *The Pro Range* – better quality products designed for professional singers and musicians.

- *Cash Sales* – to members of the public at the small factory shop.

The business is registered for VAT, and the rate charged on all items is the basic rate of 20%.

All expenditure should be analysed as you feel appropriate.

When setting the company up in Sage you should select the Financial Year as starting in April 2014. You should set the program date at 30th April 2014.

You should ensure that your name and the date appear on all print outs.

COMPANY DETAILS

Business Name	*The Exe Factory*
Proprietor	*Simeon Powell*
Address	*10 Topp Way* *Disclington* *DS77 9YH*
Telephone Number	*0845 18090982*
E-Mail	*info@exefactory.webnet.uk*
VAT Number	483876517

Task 1.1

(a) Refer to the customer details below and set up customer records to open Sales Ledger Accounts for each customer. Enter opening balances as individual amounts.

Customer details

Customer Name, Address and Contact Details	Customer Account Code	Customer Account Details
Sunshine Singalongs 10 Pavarotti Way Miltonby MB18 8FC Tel: 01927 218731 Contact: Chelsea Curle	SS001	Credit Limit = £4,000 Payment Terms = 28 days Opening Balance = £2,031.22 (relates to invoice 00146 dated 21st March 2014)
Carrie Oakey Soprano Avenue Hubley HB2 9GF Tel: 07732 389181 Contact: Carrie Oakey	CO001	Credit Limit = £10,000 Payment Terms = 28 days Opening Balance = £8,143.20 (relates to invoice 00148 dated 27th March 2014)
Poptastic Ltd Caruso Industrial Estate Mellingham ML21 9GF Tel: 07712 381912 Contact: Lewis Welsh	PP002	Credit Limit = £6,000 Payment Terms = 28 days Opening Balance = £4,132.49 (relates to invoice 00154 dated 28th March 2014 for £2,129.21 and invoice 00157 dated 31st March 2014 for £2,003.28)
Sensational Singers Ltd 10 St Bart's Row Kylie's Cross KC19 8HA Tel: 0845 217983 Contact: Dana Miload	SS002	Credit Limit = £5,000 Payment Terms = 28 days Opening Balance = £190.87 (relates to invoice 00129 dated 17th January 2014)

(b) Save your work and print a Customer Activity (Detailed) Report.

Task 1.2

Refer to the Supplier Details below and create supplier records to open Purchase Ledger Accounts for each supplier.

Supplier name, address and contact details	Supplier Account Code	Supplier Account Details
Wardshayne Ltd Unit 72 Killingham KT17 5DE Tel : 02618 1818910 Contact: Majid Singh	WD002	Credit Limit = £5000 Payment Terms = 30 days Opening Balance = £2126.37 (relates to Invoice 189 dated 18 March 2014)
Gates Ltd Birch House Wilchester WL77 4WA Tel: 07715 2781718 Contact: Jeff Little	GT003	Credit Limit = £6,000 Payment Terms= 30 days Opening Balance = £1398.18 (relates to Invoice 18918 dated 20 March 2014)
Young & Co The Lodge Lutton LT54 9PL Tel: 0845 1398232 Contact: Robin Maclay	YG001	Credit Limit = £4,000 Payment Terms = 30 days Opening Balance = £2,101.92 (relates to Invoice YG1089 dated 12 March 2014)
Brooks, Stein & Co 172 Federal Way Herdlington HR89 9WE Tel : 07119 010920 Contact: Katherine Rose	BS004	Credit Limit = £6,000 Payment Terms = 14 days Opening Balance = £1,001.29 (relates to Invoice 7326 dated 20 March 2014)
Lewis Ltd 22 Edinburgh Street Delby DL55 4CH Tel : 01928 238911 Contact: Emily Wills	LL002	Credit Limit = £1,000 Payment Terms = 30 days Opening Balance = £0.00

(c)   Save your work and print a Supplier Activity (Detailed) Report.

Task 1.3

Enter the following opening balances into the appropriate nominal accounts, making any amendments you feel are necessary.

Balances as at 1 April 2014

Account Name	£	£
Motor Vehicles	12,400.98	
Office Equipment	4,219.35	
Plant and Machinery	92,420.12	
Bank	9,218.81	
Petty Cash	200.00	
Sales Ledger Control Account*	14497.78	
Purchase Ledger Control Account*		6,627.76
VAT on Sales		15,212.61
VAT on Purchases	7,524.31	
Sales – Fun & Funky		38,120.19
Sales – Pro Range		29,108.62
Cash Sales		16,210.40
Profit & Loss Account		55,681.39
Capital		25,000.00
Rent and Rates	1,100.00	
Insurance	450.00	
Heat & Light	1729.82	
Advertising	1,480.32	
Purchases of materials	38,734.19	
Stationery	892.36	
Miscellaneous Motor Expenses	1,092.93	
	185,960.97	185,960.97

- **Note:** You do not need to enter the balances for Sales Ledger Control Account and Purchase Ledger Control Account. These totals should already be present as they represent the totals of the individual customer and supplier accounts you entered earlier.

Task 1.4

(a) Use the appropriate software tool to check for data errors.

(b) Print a screen shot of the data verification screen.

(c) Make any necessary corrections.

Task 1.5

(a) Print a trial balance.

(b) Check the accuracy of the trial balance and, if necessary, correct any errors.

Task 2.1

You have received the following e-mail from Wardshayne Ltd (a supplier).

To:	info@exefactory.webnet.uk
From:	majid@wardshayneltd.co.uk

Date: 29/03/2014

Hello

Just to let you know that we are moving! From 31st March our new address will be Blossom House, 87 Thomas Street, Catbury, CT55 3FD

Our new phone number is 0845 6712821

Please ensure that you update all records with this change in address

Kind regards, and thank you for your continued support

Majid

(a) Print a screen shot of the supplier's record with the current address and telephone number.

(b) Enter the new address and telephone number into the accounting system.

(c) Print a screen shot of the supplier's details with the amended address and telephone number.

Task 2.2

Refer to the following sales invoices and credit note:

The ExeFactory
10 Topp Way

Disclington

DS77 9YH
"The Best Microphones, The Best Value"

INVOICE 00160
Tax Point : 1ˢᵗ April 2014   VAT Registration Number: 483876517

Carrie Oakey
Soprano Avenue
Hubley
HB2 9GF

Fun & Funky × 3	£30.00	£90.00
Pro Range × 1	£99.00	£99.00
		£189.00
VAT @ 20%		£37.80
TOTAL FOR PAYMENT		£226.80

Terms: 30 days

173

The ExeFactory
10 Topp Way

Disclington

DS77 9YH
"The Best Microphones, The Best Value"

INVOICE 00162
Tax Point : 1st April 2014　　　　　　VAT Registration Number: 483876517

Poptastic Ltd
Caruso Industrial Estate
Mellingham
ML21 9GF

Pro Range × 7	£99.00	£693.00
		£693.00
VAT @ 20%		£138.60
TOTAL FOR PAYMENT		£831.60

Terms: 30 days

The ExeFactory
10 Topp Way

Disclington

DS77 9YH
"The Best Microphones, The Best Value"

INVOICE 00163
Tax Point : 5th April 2014   VAT Registration Number: 483876517

Sunshine Singalongs
10 Pavarotti Way
Miltonby
MB18 8FC

Fun & Funky × 8	£30.00	£240.00
Pro Range × 10	£99.00	£990.00
		£1230.00
VAT @ 20%		£246.00
TOTAL FOR PAYMENT		£1476.00

Terms: 30 days

The ExeFactory

10 Topp Way

Disclington

DS77 9YH
"The Best Microphones, The Best Value"

CREDIT NOTE 41
Tax Point : 2nd April 2014   VAT Registration Number: 483876517

Carrie Oakey
Soprano Avenue
Hubley
HB2 9GF

Pro Range × 1 (Faulty Goods)	£99.00	£99.00
VAT @ 20%		£19.80
		_____
TOTAL FOR PAYMENT		£118.80

Terms: 30 days

(a)   Enter the sales invoices and credit notes into the computerised accounting system.

Refer to the following summary of purchase invoices:

Date	Supplier	Invoice No	Gross £	VAT £	Net £	Materials	Accountancy
3/4/14	Young & Co	YG1120	307.90	51.32	256.58		256.58
4/4/14	Lewis Ltd	1918	423.00	70.50	352.50	352.50	
5/4/14	Wardshayne Ltd	218	94.00	15.67	78.33	78.33	
	Totals		824.89	137.48	687.41	430.83	256.58

(b)   Enter the purchase invoices into the computerised accounting system.

Refer to the following summary of payments received from customers and made to suppliers:

Cheque / BACS Receipts Listing

Date	Details	Customer	£	How Received
04 Apr 14	Payment of opening balance	Carrie Oakey	8143.20	BACS
05 Apr 14	Payment of opening balance	Sunshine Singalongs	2031.22	CHEQUE

Cheques Paid Listing

Date	Details	Supplier	£	Cheque Number
04 Apr 14	Payment of opening balance	Young & Co	2101.92	001301
04 Apr 14	Payment of opening balance	Wardshayne Ltd	2126.37	001302

(c)   Enter the receipts and payments into the computer, making sure you allocate all amounts as shown in the details column.

Refer to the following email from Simeon:

---

email

From : Simeon@Simeontimbercrafts.co.uk

To : accounts@Simeontimbercrafts.co.uk

Date: 5 April 2014

Subject: Poptastic Ltd

Hi

I'm afraid that Poptastic Ltd have gone into liquidation – I've just had a letter from their administrators. It looks most unlikely we will get anything for their outstanding account.

Please let me know how much they owe us, and then write this amount off as a bad debt.

Thanks

Simeon

(d)   Print a customer statement for Poptastic Ltd, showing the balance currently owed. Then make the entries into the computer to write off the amount owing from Poptastic Ltd. Ignore VAT. Print a new customer statement showing the amount written off and the new balance of nil.

Task 2.3

Refer to the following petty cash vouchers:

Petty Cash Voucher	
Date 3 April 2014 Ref: PC 22	
Details	
Window cleaner (*zero rated for VAT purposes*) Receipt attached	£15.00

Petty Cash Voucher	
Date 6 April 2014 Ref: PC 23	
Details	
Pot plants for reception	£31.21
VAT	£6.24
Total	£37.45
Receipt attached	

Enter the petty cash payments into the computer. Code the purchase of pot plants to Nominal Code 7803.

Task 2.4

Refer to the following receipts issued for cash sales in the factory shop: you should assume that the monies are banked in the current account immediately.

Receipt	Receipt
No: 369	No: 370
2nd April 2014	6th April 2014
Received by cheque	Received by cheque
£30.00 excluding VAT	£232.65 including VAT

(a)   Enter these receipts in the computer.

Refer to the following email from Simeon:

email

From : simeon@exefactory.webnet.uk

To : accounts@exefactory.webnet.uk

Date: 3 April 2014

Subject: Donation

Hi

Just to let you know that I took £25 out of the bank account this morning and made a donation to a local school.

Thanks

Simeon

(b)   Enter this transaction in the computer.

Task 2.5

Refer to the following email from Simeon:

email
From : simeon@exefactory.webnet.uk
To : accounts@exefactory.webnet.uk
Date: 6 April 2014
Subject: Opening Balances

Hi

I've just realised that the list of opening balances I gave you for entry to the new computer system contained an error. The balance of £450.00 for insurance actually contains a sum of £80.00 which should be classified as Advertising – sorry, my mistake!

Could you please correct this for me?

Thanks

Simeon

Enter the appropriate journal into the computer to correct the error in the opening balances.

Task 2.6

(a)   Print a screen shot of the journal.

Task 2.7

(a)   Print a trial balance.

(b)   Check the accuracy of the trial balance and, if necessary, correct any errors.

Task 3.1

Refer to the following email from Simeon:

email
From : Simeon@exefactory.webnet.uk
To : accounts@exefactory.webnet.uk
Date: 8 April 2014
Subject: New customer

Hi

Could you please enter the details of a new customer that I have agreed terms with this morning?

The details are:

Boyles Ltd

20 Byways Lane

Grasston

GR44 6CB

The contact name is Susan Verity

The settlement terms are 14 days with a credit limit of £2,000.

Please select an appropriate Customer Account Code for this customer

Thanks

Simeon

(a) Set up a new customer record for Boyles Ltd to open a sales ledger account with an opening balance of nil.

(b) Print a screen shot of the new customer's record card showing the name and address details.

Task 3.2

Refer to the following sales invoices:

The ExeFactory
10 Topp Way

Disclington

DS77 9YH

"The Best Microphones, The Best Value"

INVOICE 00164
Tax Point : 6th April 2014
VAT Registration Number: 483876517

Carrie Oakey

Soprano Avenue

Hubley

HB2 9GF

Fun & Funky × 5	£30.00	£150.00
Pro Range × 5	£90.00	£450.00
		£600.00
VAT @ 20%		£120.00
TOTAL FOR PAYMENT		£720.00

Terms: 14 days

The ExeFactory

10 Topp Way

Disclington

DS77 9YH
"The Best Microphones, The Best Value"

INVOICE 00165
Tax Point : 6th April 2014
VAT Registration Number: 483876517

Boyles Ltd

20 Byways Lane

Grasston

GR44 6CB

Pro Range × 8	£90.00	£720.00
		£720.00
VAT @ 20%		£144.00
TOTAL FOR PAYMENT		£864.00

Terms: 14 days

(a)   Enter the sales invoices into the computer.

Refer to the following summary of purchases invoices:

Date	Supplier Name	Invoice Number	Gross £	VAT £	Net £	Materials £	Advertising £
8/4/14	Brooks, Stein & Co	7398	1175.00	195.83	979.17		979.17
10/4/14	Lewis Ltd	LW1054	658.00	109.67	548.33	548.33	
		Total	**1833.00**	**305.50**	**1527.50**	**548.33**	**979.17**

(b) Enter the purchase invoices into the computer.

Refer to the following summary of payments received from customers and made to suppliers:

Cheque / BACS Receipts Listing

Date	Details	Customer	£	How Received
11/4/14	Payment of Invoice 00160 including credit note CN41	Carrie Oakey	108.00	BACS

Cheques Paid Listing

Date	Details	Supplier	£	Cheque Number
12/4/14	Payment of opening balance	Gates Ltd	1398.18	001302
12/4/14	Part-payment of opening balance	Brooks, Stein & Co	500.00	001303

(c) Enter the receipts and payments into the computer, making sure you allocate all amounts as shown in the details column.

Task 3.3

Refer to the following petty cash vouchers:

Petty Cash Voucher

Date 12 April 2014
Ref: PC 24

Details	
Train fare – exempt for VAT	£22.60
Receipt attached	

Petty Cash Voucher

Date 14 April 2014
Ref: PC 25

Details	
Printer cartridge	£19.99
VAT	£4.00
	———
Total	£23.99
	———
Receipt attached	

Enter the petty cash payments into the computer.

Task 3.4

Refer to the following e-mail from Simeon:

---

email

From : Simeon@Simeontimbercrafts.co.uk

To : accounts@Simeontimbercrafts.co.uk

Date: 14 April 2014

Subject: Grant

Hi

I don't know if you remember me telling you but I applied for a grant a few months ago – and guess what! We've just got a cheque through from the grant agency for £300 – I've taken it to the bank this morning when I was passing.

Could you enter it into the system please?

Thanks

Simeon

(a)   Enter this grant income into the computer.

Refer to the following receipt for the purchase of a new picture, paid for out of petty cash:

Receipt Number 1331

Art of the Matter

Kitchener Shopping Centre

Miltonby

VAT Reg: 343 4839 47

Date : 14 April 2014

Received from Simeon Powell, by cash, for original print

£60 inc VAT

(b)   Enter the details of this transaction into the computer. This is a picture for the office wall, so should be coded to Nominal Code 7803.

Refer to the following schedule of standing orders:

Day in month	Payee	Expense	£
15th	J Jones	Rent	500.00
16th	Disclington B. C.	Rates	160.00

Assume both of these are zero-rated.

(c)   Enter the standing orders into the computer as recurring transactions being taken from the bank on the 15th of each month, and post them as necessary to ensure that April's transactions are entered into the computer.

Task 3.5

Refer to the post-it note left on your desk by Simeon shown below:

Hi

Sorry – the grant was for £350, not £300 as I said.

Simeon

Adjust the figure by making appropriate entries to the bank account.

Task 3.6

Refer to the email below from Simeon:

email
From : Simeon@exefactory.webnet.uk
To : accounts@exefactory.webnet.uk
Date: 30th April 2014
Subject: Petty cash

Hi

Please transfer the correct amount from the bank account to the petty cash account to reimburse the petty cash float – this should reinstate it to £200.00.

Thanks

Simeon

(a)   Enter this transaction into the computer.

(b)   Print the cash payments record for the petty cash account.

Task 3.7

(a)   Print a trial balance.

(b)   Check the accuracy of the trial balance and, if necessary, correct any errors.

Task 4.1

(a)   Back up your work to a suitable storage media.

(b)   Print a screen shot of the backup screen showing the location of back up data.

Task 4.2

Print the following reports:

(a)   The customer invoices overdue report

(b)   The customer activity (detailed) report

(c)   The purchases day book (supplier invoices)

Task 4.3

(a)   Generate an Aged Creditor Analysis showing all outstanding items and print a copy.

(b)   Generate an Aged Debtors Analysis showing all outstanding items and print a copy.

Task 4.4

Print a Statement of Account for Carrie Oakey.

2 Practice Assessment Answers

Task 1.1

Customer Activity (Detailed) Report

Date:	22/04/2014	The Exe Factory	Page: 1
Time:	12:53:08	Customer Activity (Detailed)	

Date From:	01/01/1980		Customer From:	
Date To:	30/04/2014		Customer To:	ZZZZZZZZ
Transaction From:	1		N/C From:	
Transaction To:	99,999,999		N/C To:	99999999
Inc b/fwd transaction:	No		Dept From:	0
Exc later payment:	No		Dept To:	999

** NOTE: All report values are shown in Base Currency, unless otherwise indicated **

A/C: CO001   Name: Carrie Oakey   Contact: Carrie Oakey   Tel: 07732 389181

No	Type	Date	Ref	N/C	Details	Dept	T/C	Value	O/S	Debit	Credit	V	B
2	SI	27/03/2014	00148	9998	Opening Balance	0	T9	8,143.20 *	8,143.20	8,143.20		-	-
							Totals:	8,143.20	8,143.20	8,143.20			

Amount Outstanding	8,143.20
Amount Paid this period	0.00
Credit Limit £	10,000.00
Turnover YTD	0.00

A/C: PP002   Name: Poptastic Ltd   Contact: Lewis Walsh   Tel: 07712 381912

No	Type	Date	Ref	N/C	Details	Dept	T/C	Value	O/S	Debit	Credit	V	B
3	SI	28/03/2014	00154	9998	Opening Balance	0	T9	2,129.21 *	2,129.21	2,129.21		-	-
4	SI	31/03/2014	00157	9998	Opening Balance	0	T9	2,003.28 *	2,003.28	2,003.28		-	-
							Totals:	4,132.49	4,132.49	4,132.49			

Amount Outstanding	4,132.49
Amount Paid this period	0.00
Credit Limit £	6,000.00
Turnover YTD	0.00

A/C: SS001   Name: Sunshine Singalongs   Contact: Chelsea Curle   Tel: 01927 218731

No	Type	Date	Ref	N/C	Details	Dept	T/C	Value	O/S	Debit	Credit	V	B
1	SI	21/03/2014	00146	9998	Opening Balance	0	T9	2,031.22 *	2,031.22	2,031.22		-	-
							Totals:	2,031.22	2,031.22	2,031.22			

Amount Outstanding	2,031.22
Amount Paid this period	0.00
Credit Limit £	4,000.00
Turnover YTD	0.00

A/C: SS002   Name: Sensational Singers Ltd   Contact: Dana Miload   Tel: 0845 217983

No	Type	Date	Ref	N/C	Details	Dept	T/C	Value	O/S	Debit	Credit	V	B
5	SI	17/03/2014	00128	9998	Opening Balance	0	T9	190.87 *	190.87	190.87		-	-
							Totals:	190.87	190.87	190.87			

Amount Outstanding	190.87
Amount Paid this period	0.00
Credit Limit £	5,000.00
Turnover YTD	0.00

Task 1.2

Date: 22/04/2014
Time: 12:35:42

The Exe Factory
Customer Activity (Detailed)

Page: 1

Date From:	01/01/1980
Date To:	30/04/2014
Transaction From:	1
Transaction To:	99,999,999
Inc b/fwd transaction:	No
Exc later payment:	No

Customer From:	
Customer To:	ZZZZZZZZ
N/C From:	
N/C To:	99999999
Dept From:	0
Dept To:	999

** NOTE: All report values are shown in Base Currency, unless otherwise indicated **

A/C: CO001 Name: Carrie Oakly   Contact: Carrie Oakley   Tel: 07732 389181

No	Type	Date	Ref	N/C	Details	Dept	T/C	Value	O/S	Debit	Credit	V	B
2	SI	27/03/2014	00148	9998	Opening Balance	0	T9	8,143.20 *	8,143.20	8,143.20		-	-
							Totals:	8,143.20	8,143.20	8,143.20			

Amount Outstanding 8,143.20
Amount Paid this period 0.00
Credit Limit £ 10,000.00
Turnover YTD 0.00

A/C: PP002 Name: Poptastic Ltd   Contact: Lewis Welsh   Tel: 07712 381912

No	Type	Date	Ref	N/C	Details	Dept	T/C	Value	O/S	Debit	Credit	V	B
3	SI	28/03/2014	00154	9998	Opening Balance	0	T9	2,129.21 *	2,129.21	2,129.21		-	-
4	SI	31/03/2014	00157	9998	Opening Balance	0	T9	2,003.28 *	2,003.28	2,003.28		-	-
							Totals:	4,132.49	4,132.49	4,132.49			

Amount Outstanding 4,132.49
Amount Paid this period 0.00
Credit Limit £ 6,000.00
Turnover YTD 0.00

A/C: SS001 Name: Sunshine Singalongs   Contact: Chelsea Curle   Tel: 01927 218731

No	Type	Date	Ref	N/C	Details	Dept	T/C	Value	O/S	Debit	Credit	V	B
1	SI	21/03/2014	00146	9998	Opening Balance	0	T9	2,031.22 *	2,031.22	2,031.22		-	-
							Totals:	2,031.22	2,031.22	2,031.22			

Amount Outstanding 2,031.22
Amount Paid this period 0.00
Credit Limit £ 4,000.00
Turnover YTD 0.00

A/C: SS002 Name: Sensational Singers Ltd   Contact: Dana Miload   Tel: 0845 217983

No	Type	Date	Ref	N/C	Details	Dept	T/C	Value	O/S	Debit	Credit	V	B
5	SI	17/03/2014	00128	9998	Opening Balance	0	T9	190.87 *	190.87	190.87		-	-
							Totals:	190.87	190.87	190.87			

Amount Outstanding 190.87
Amount Paid this period 0.00
Credit Limit £ 5,000.00
Turnover YTD 0.00

Task 1.3

This is a data input task so no answer given.

Task 1.4

Task 1.5

Date: 22/04/2014		The Exe Factory	Page: 1
Time: 12:47:24		**Period Trial Balance**	

To Period: Month 12, March 2015

N/C	Name	Debit	Credit
0020	Plant and Machinery	92,420.12	
0030	Office Equipment	4,219.35	
0050	Motor Vehicles	12,400.98	
1100	Debtors Control Account	14,497.78	
1200	Bank Current Account	9,218.81	
1230	Petty Cash	200.00	
2100	Creditors Control Account		6,627.76
2200	Sales Tax Control Account		15,212.61
2201	Purchase Tax Control Account	7,524.31	
3000	Capital		25,000.00
3200	Profit and Loss Account		55,681.39
4000	Sales - Fun & Funky		38,120.19
4001	Sales - Pro Range		29,108.62
4002	Cash sales		16,210.40
5000	Materials Purchased	38,734.19	
6201	Advertising	1,480.32	
7100	Rent and rates	1,100.00	
7200	Heat and light	1,729.82	
7304	Miscellaneous Motor Expenses	1,092.93	
7500	Staionery	892.36	
8204	Insurance	450.00	
	Totals:	185,960.97	185,960.97

Task 2.1 (a)

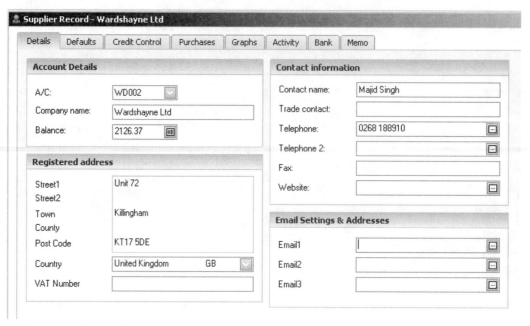

Task 2.1 (c)

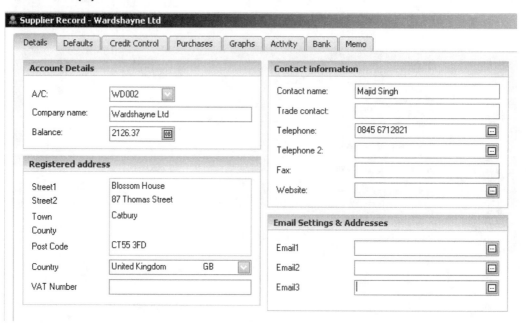

Task 2.2 (d)

The Exe Factory
10 Topp Way
Disclington
DS77 9YH

Poptastic Ltd   PP002
Caruso Industrial Estate
Mellingham   30/04/2014
ML21 9GF
                                        1

NOTE: All values are shown in Pound Sterling

8/03/14 00154	Goods/Services	2,129.21 *
1/03/14 00157	Goods/Services	2,003.28 *
1/04/14 00162	Goods/Services	831.60 *

The Exe Factory
10 Topp Way
Disclington
DS77 9YH

Poptastic Ltd   PP002
Caruso Industrial Estate
Mellingham   30/04/2014
ML21 9GF
                                        1

NOTE: All values are shown in Pound Sterling

28/03/14	Goods/Services	2,129.21
31/03/14	Goods/Services	2,003.28
01/04/14	Goods/Services	831.60

831.60 £   4,132.49 £   0.00 £   0.00 £   0.00

£ 4,964.09   £ 4,964.09

The Exe Factory
10 Topp Way
Disclington
DS77 9YH

Poptastic Ltd
Caruso Industrial Estate
Mellingham
ML21 9GF

PPO02

30/04/2014

1

NOTE: All values are shown in Pound Sterling

28/03/14	00154	Goods/Services	2,129.21	
31/03/14	00157	Goods/Services	2,003.28	
01/04/14	00162	Goods/Services	831.60	
05/04/14	BADDB	Credit		2,129.21
05/04/14	BADDB	Credit		2,003.28
05/04/14	BADDB	Credit		831.60

£ 0.00 £ 0.00 £ 0.00 £ 0.00 £ 0.00

£ 0.00

The Exe Factory
10 Topp Way
Disclington
DS77 9YH

Poptastic Ltd
Caruso Industrial Estate
Mellingham
ML21 9GF

PP002

30/04/2014

1

NOTE: All values are shown in Pound Sterling

28/03/14	Goods/Services	2,129.21	
31/03/14	Goods/Services	2,003.28	
01/04/14	Goods/Services	831.60	
05/04/14	Credit		2,129.21
05/04/14	Credit		2,003.28
05/04/14	Credit		831.60

£ 0.00

KAPLAN PUBLISHING

Task 2.6

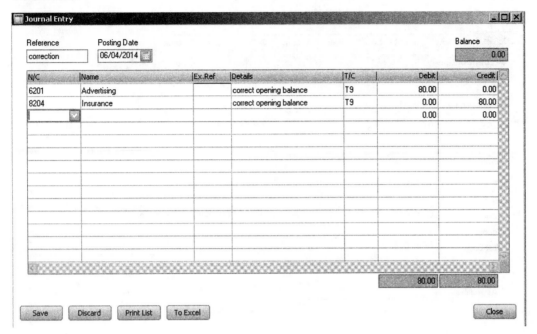

Task 2.7

Date: 22/04/2014   **The Exe Factory**   **Page:** 1
Time: 13:14:54   **Period Trial Balance**

To Period: Month 12, March 2015

N/C	Name	Debit	Credit
0020	Plant and Machinery	92,420.12	
0030	Office Equipment	4,219.35	
0050	Motor Vehicles	12,400.98	
1100	Debtors Control Account	1,774.87	
1200	Bank Current Account	15,408.59	
1230	Petty Cash	147.55	
2100	Creditors Control Account		3,224.37
2200	Sales Tax Control Account		15,659.98
2201	Purchase Tax Control Account	7,668.04	
3000	Capital		25,000.00
3200	Profit and Loss Account		55,681.39
4000	Sales - Fun & Funky		38,450.19
4001	Sales - Pro Range		30,791.62
4002	Cash sales		16,434.28
5000	Materials Purchased	39,165.02	
6201	Advertising	1,560.32	
7100	Rent and rates	1,100.00	
7200	Heat and light	1,729.82	
7304	Miscellaneous Motor Expenses	1,092.93	
7500	Staionery	892.36	
7602	Accountancy Fees	256.58	
7801	Cleaning	15.00	
7803	Premises Expenses	31.21	
8100	Bad Debt Write Off	4,964.09	
8200	Donations	25.00	
8204	Insurance	370.00	
	Totals:	185,241.83	185,241.83

Task 3.1

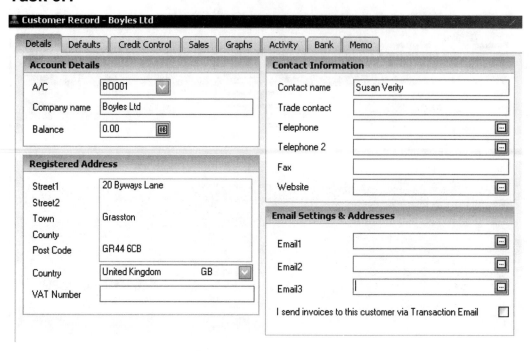

Customer Record - Boyles Ltd

Details | Defaults | Credit Control | Sales | Graphs | Activity | Bank | Memo

Account Details

A/C	BO001
Company name	Boyles Ltd
Balance	0.00 [OB]

Registered Address

Street1	20 Byways Lane
Street2	
Town	Grasston
County	
Post Code	GR44 6CB
Country	United Kingdom GB
VAT Number	

Contact Information

Contact name	Susan Verity
Trade contact	
Telephone	
Telephone 2	
Fax	
Website	

Email Settings & Addresses

Email1	
Email2	
Email3	

I send invoices to this customer via Transaction Email ☐

Task 3.6

Date: 22/04/2014				**The Exe Factory**					**Page:** 1	
Time: 13:38:30				**Day Books: Cash Payments (Detailed)**						

Date From:	01/01/1980	**Bank From:**	1230
Date To:	31/12/2019	**Bank To:**	1230
Transaction From:	1	**N/C From:**	
Transaction To:	99,999,999	**N/C To:**	99999999
Dept From:	0		
Dept To:	999		

Bank: 1230   **Currency:** Pound Sterling

No	Type	N/C	Date	Ref	Details	Dept	Net £	Tax £	T/C	Gross £	V	B	Bank Rec. Date
66	CP	7801	03/04/2014	PC22	windows	0	15.00	0.00	T0	15.00	N	-	
67	CP	7803	06/04/2014	PC23	Pot plants	0	31.21	6.24	T1	37.45	N	-	
81	CP	7400	12/04/2014	PC24	train fare	0	22.60	0.00	T9	22.60	-	-	
82	CP	7500	14/04/2014	PC25	cartridge	0	19.99	4.00	T1	23.99	N	-	
84	CP	7803	14/04/2014	1331	picture	0	50.00	10.00	T1	60.00	N	-	
					Totals £		138.80	20.24		159.04			

Task 3.7

Date: 22/04/2014
Time: 13:39:41

The Exe Factory
Period Trial Balance

Page: 1

To Period: Month 12, March 2015

N/C	Name	Debit	Credit
0020	Plant and Machinery	92,420.12	
0030	Office Equipment	4,219.35	
0050	Motor Vehicles	12,400.98	
1100	Debtors Control Account	3,250.87	
1200	Bank Current Account	13,149.37	
1230	Petty Cash	200.00	
2100	Creditors Control Account		3,159.19
2200	Sales Tax Control Account		15,923.98
2201	Purchase Tax Control Account	7,987.54	
3000	Capital		25,000.00
3200	Profit and Loss Account		55,681.39
4000	Sales - Fun & Funky		38,600.19
4001	Sales - Pro Range		31,961.62
4002	Cash sales		16,434.28
4900	Miscellaneous Income		350.00
5000	Materials Purchased	39,713.35	
6201	Advertising	2,539.49	
7100	Rent and rates	1,760.00	
7200	Heat and light	1,729.82	
7304	Miscellaneous Motor Expenses	1,092.93	
7400	Travelling	22.60	
7500	Staionery	912.35	
7602	Accountancy Fees	256.58	
7801	Cleaning	15.00	
7803	Premises Expenses	81.21	
8100	Bad Debt Write Off	4,964.09	
8200	Donations	25.00	
8204	Insurance	370.00	
	Totals:	**187,110.65**	**187,110.65**

Task 4.1 (a)

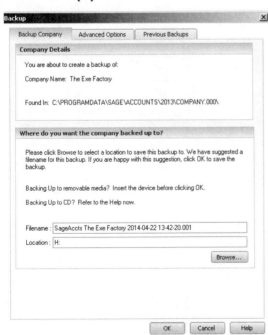

Task 4.1 (b)

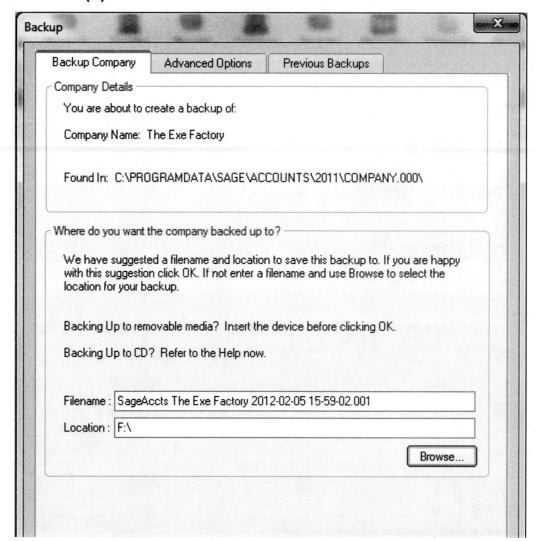

Task 4.2(a)

Date:	22/04/2014		The Exe Factory		Page:	1
Time:	14:01:13		Customer Invoices Overdue			

Customer From:				Date From:	01/01/1980
Customer To:	ZZZZZZZ			Date To:	30/04/2014
Transaction From:	1			Exc Later Payments:	No
Transaction To:	99,999,999				

A/C:	BO001	Name:	Boyles Ltd		Contact:	Susan Verity		Tel:	

No	Type	Date	Due Date	Ref	Details	Amount	Paid	Outstanding
75	SI	06/04/2014	20/04/2014	00165		864.00	0.00	864.00
							Total:	864.00

A/C:	CO001	Name:	Carrie Oakey		Contact:	Carrie Oakey		Tel:	07732 389181

No	Type	Date	Due Date	Ref	Details	Amount	Paid	Outstanding
50	SI	01/04/2014	29/04/2014	00160		226.80	108.00	118.80
							Total:	118.80

A/C:	SS002	Name:	Sensational Singers Ltd		Contact:	Dana Miload		Tel:	0845 217983

No	Type	Date	Due Date	Ref	Details	Amount	Paid	Outstanding
5	SI	17/03/2014	14/04/2014	00128	Opening Balance	190.87	0.00	190.87
							Total:	190.87
							Grand Total:	1,173.67

Task 4.2(b)

Date:	22/04/2014		The Exe Factory		Page:	1
Time:	14:03:36		Customer Activity (Detailed)			

Date From:	01/01/1980			Customer From:	
Date To:	30/04/2014			Customer To:	ZZZZZZZZ
Transaction From:	1			N/C From:	
Transaction To:	99,999,999			N/C To:	99999999
Inc b/fwd transaction:	No			Dept From:	0
Exc later payment:	No			Dept To:	999

** NOTE: All report values are shown in Base Currency, unless otherwise indicated **

A/C:	BO001	Name:	Boyles Ltd		Contact:	Susan Verity		Tel:	

No	Type	Date	Ref	N/C	Details	Dept	T/C	Value	O/S	Debit	Credit	V	B
75	SI	06/04/2014	00165	4001		0	T1	864.00 *	864.00	864.00		N	-
							Totals:	864.00	864.00	864.00			

Amount Outstanding	864.00
Amount Paid this period	0.00
Credit Limit £	2,000.00
Turnover YTD	720.00

A/C:	CO001	Name:	Carrie Oakey		Contact:	Carrie Oakey		Tel:	07732 389181

No	Type	Date	Ref	N/C	Details	Dept	T/C	Value	O/S	Debit	Credit	V	B
2	SI	27/03/2014	00148	9998	Opening Balance	0	T9	8,143.20		8,143.20		-	-
50	SI	01/04/2014	00160	4000		0	T1	108.00		108.00		N	-
51	SI	01/04/2014	00160	4001		0	T1	118.80 *	118.80	118.80		N	-
55	SC	30/04/2014	41	4001	faulty goods	0	T1	118.80 *	-118.80		118.80	N	-
59	SR	04/04/2014	BACS	1200	Sales Receipt	0	T9	8,143.20			8,143.20	-	N
73	SI	06/04/2014	00164	4000		0	T1	180.00 *	180.00	180.00		N	-
74	SI	06/04/2014	00164	4001		0	T1	540.00 *	540.00	540.00		N	-
78	SR	11/04/2014	BACS	1200	Sales Receipt	0	T9	108.00			108.00	-	N
							Totals:	720.00	720.00	9,090.00	8,370.00		

Amount Outstanding	720.00
Amount Paid this period	8,251.20
Credit Limit £	10,000.00
Turnover YTD	690.00

A/C:	PP002	Name:	Poptastic Ltd		Contact:	Lewis Welsh		Tel:	07712 381912

No	Type	Date	Ref	N/C	Details	Dept	T/C	Value	O/S	Debit	Credit	V	B
3	SI	28/03/2014	00154	9998	Opening Balance	0	T9	2,129.21		2,129.21		-	-
4	SI	31/03/2014	00157	9998	Opening Balance	0	T9	2,003.28		2,003.28		-	-
52	SI	01/04/2014	00162	4001		0	T1	831.60		831.60		N	-
63	SC	05/04/2014	BADDBT	8100	Bad Debt Write Off	0	T9	2,129.21			2,129.21	-	-
64	SC	05/04/2014	BADDBT	8100	Bad Debt Write Off	0	T9	2,003.28			2,003.28	-	-
65	SC	05/04/2014	BADDBT	8100	Bad Debt Write Off	0	T9	831.60			831.60	-	-
							Totals:	0.00	0.00	4,964.09	4,964.09		

A/C:	SS001	**Name:**	Sunshine Singalongs			**Contact:**	Chelsea Curle				**Tel:**	01927 218731		

No	Type	Date	Ref	N/C	Details	Dept	T/C	Value	O/S	Debit	Credit	V	B
1	SI	21/03/2014	00146	9998	Opening Balance	0	T9	2,031.22		2,031.22		-	-
53	SI	05/04/2014	00163	4000		0	T1	288.00 *	288.00	288.00		N	-
54	SI	05/04/2014	00163	4001		0	T1	1,188.00 *	1,188.00	1,188.00		N	-
60	SR	05/04/2014	Cheque	1200	Sales Receipt	0	T9	2,031.22			2,031.22	-	N
						Totals:		1,476.00	1,476.00	3,507.22	2,031.22		

Amount Outstanding	1,476.00
Amount Paid this period	2,031.22
Credit Limit £	4,000.00
Turnover YTD	1,230.00

Date: 22/04/2014
Time: 14:03:36

The Exe Factory
Customer Activity (Detailed)

Page: 2

A/C:	SS002	**Name:**	Sensational Singers Ltd			**Contact:**	Dana Miload				**Tel:**	0845 217983		

No	Type	Date	Ref	N/C	Details	Dept	T/C	Value	O/S	Debit	Credit	V	B
5	SI	17/03/2014	00128	9998	Opening Balance	0	T9	190.87 *	190.87	190.87		-	-
						Totals:		190.87	190.87	190.87			

Amount Outstanding	190.87
Amount Paid this period	0.00
Credit Limit £	5,000.00
Turnover YTD	0.00

Task 4.2(c)

Date: 22/04/2014
Time: 14:09:46

The Exe Factory
Day Books: Supplier Invoices (Detailed)

Page: 1

Date From:	01/01/1980	**Supplier From:**	
Date To:	31/12/2019	**Supplier To:**	ZZZZZZZZ
Transaction From:	1	**N/C From:**	
Transaction To:	99,999,999	**N/C To:**	99999999
Dept From:	0		
Dept To:	999		

Tran No.	Type	Date	A/C Ref	N/C	Inv Ref	Dept	Details	Net Amount	Tax Amount	T/C	Gross Amount	V	B
6	PI	18/03/2014	WD002	9998	189	0	Opening Balance	2,126.37	0.00	T9	2,126.37	-	-
7	PI	20/03/2014	GT003	9998	18918	0	Opening Balance	1,398.18	0.00	T9	1,398.18	-	-
8	PI	12/03/2014	YG001	9998	YG1089	0	Opening Balance	2,101.92	0.00	T9	2,101.92	-	-
9	PI	20/03/2014	BS004	9998	7326	0	Opening Balance	1,001.29	0.00	T9	1,001.29	-	-
56	PI	03/04/2014	YG001	7602	YG1120	0		256.58	51.32	T1	307.90	N	-
57	PI	04/04/2014	LL002	5000	1918	0		352.50	70.50	T1	423.00	N	-
58	PI	05/04/2014	WD002	5000	218	0		78.33	15.67	T1	94.00	N	-
76	PI	08/04/2014	BS004	6201	7398	0		979.17	195.83	T1	1,175.00	N	-
77	PI	10/04/2014	LL002	5000	LW1054	0		548.33	109.67	T1	658.00	N	-
							Totals	8,842.67	442.99		9,285.66		

Task 4.3(a)

Date:	22/04/2014				The Exe Factory						Page:	1
Time:	14:11:05				**Aged Creditors Analysis (Summary)**							

Report Date:	30/04/2014	Supplier From:
Include future transactions:	No	Supplier To: ZZZZZZZ
Exclude Later Payments:	No	

** NOTE: All report values are shown in Base Currency, unless otherwise indicated **

A/C	Name	Credit Limit	Turnover	Balance	Future	Current	Period 1	Period 2	Period 3	Older
BS004	Brooks, Stein & Co	£ 6,000.00	979.17	1,676.29	0.00	1,175.00	501.29	0.00	0.00	0.00
LL002	Lewis Ltd	£ 1,000.00	900.83	1,081.00	0.00	1,081.00	0.00	0.00	0.00	0.00
WD002	Wardshayne Ltd	£ 5,000.00	78.33	94.00	0.00	94.00	0.00	0.00	0.00	0.00
YG001	Young & Co	£ 4,000.00	256.58	307.90	0.00	307.90	0.00	0.00	0.00	0.00
	Totals:		2,214.91	3,159.19	0.00	2,657.90	501.29	0.00	0.00	0.00

Task 4.3(b)

Date:	22/04/2014				The Exe Factory						Page:	1
Time:	14:11:54				**Aged Debtors Analysis (Summary)**							

Report Date:	30/04/2014	Customer From:
Include future transactions:	No	Customer To: ZZZZZZZ
Exclude later payments:	No	

** NOTE: All report values are shown in Base Currency, unless otherwise indicated **

A/C	Name	Credit Limit	Turnover	Balance	Future	Current	Period 1	Period 2	Period 3	Older
BO001	Boyles Ltd	£ 2,000.00	720.00	864.00	0.00	864.00	0.00	0.00	0.00	0.00
CO001	Carrie Oakey	£ 10,000.00	690.00	720.00	0.00	720.00	0.00	0.00	0.00	0.00
SS001	Sunshine Singalongs	£ 4,000.00	1,230.00	1,476.00	0.00	1,476.00	0.00	0.00	0.00	0.00
SS002	Sensational Singers Ltd	£ 5,000.00	0.00	190.87	0.00	0.00	190.87	0.00	0.00	0.00
	Totals:		2,640.00	3,250.87	0.00	3,060.00	190.87	0.00	0.00	0.00

Task 4.4

The Exe Factory				The Exe Factory			
10 Topp Way				10 Topp Way			
Disclington				Disclington			
DS77 9YH				DS77 9YH			

Carrie Oakey	CO001		Carrie Oakey	CO001	
Soprano Avenue			Soprano Avenue		
Hubley	30/04/2014		Hubley	30/04/2014	
HB2 9GF			HB2 9GF		
	1			1	

NOTE: All values are shown in Pound Sterling   **NOTE: All values are shown in Pound Sterling**

27/03/14 00148	Goods/Services	8,143.20			
01/04/14 00160	Goods/Services	226.80 p			
30/04/14 41	Credit	*	118.80		
04/04/14 BACS	Payment		8,143.20		
06/04/14 00164	Goods/Services	720.00 *			
11/04/14 BACS	Payment		108.00		

27/03/14	Goods/Services	8,143.20			
01/04/14	Goods/Services	226.80			
30/04/14	Credit		118.80		
04/04/14	Payment		8,143.20		
06/04/14	Goods/Services	720.00			
11/04/14	Payment		108.00		

£ 720.00 £ 0.00 £ 0.00 £ 0.00 £ 0.00

£ 720.00   £ 720.00

INDEX

KAPLAN PUBLISHING